# My Life and Times

# My Life and Times

## Reflections of a Bit Player on Our Modern Times

## S.R. Leonard

**To order additional copies of this book, contact:**
Xlibris Corporation
1-888-795-4274
www.Xlibris.com
Orders@Xlibris.com
27591

# Contents

# Acknowledgments

It is with great thanks that I give credit to some of those who have helped me bring this book to fruition. In this day of computerized writing and digital publishing, I have benefited from the expertise of several individuals, in particular. To my friends John Fortier and John Daley, I extend thanks for help with the details of indexing and general advice relating to word processing. Thanks are also due to Monica Chartier of Teck Solutions for helping repair and retrieve lost files and computer malfunctions. I am also grateful to Clayton Shaker and Jill Dolphin for their facile handling of the details of imaging files and text preparation. They helped to make the final submission files correct and complete.

As in many of the undertakings in my life, I thank especially my dear wife Kristine for her wise counsel and help. Her considerable knowledge of the rudiments of writing and expression in the English language has been invaluable in editing the manuscript and in helping me to reach the mark that I set out to achieve. Furthermore, her sense of proportion and aesthetics has been fundamental in the aspects of layout, cover design and the appearance of the final text. I have kept her busy with these details and I love her and appreciate her for the time it has taken in her life.

Finally, I thank the staff at Xlibris for their kind attention and work in making my writings into the book that I envisioned at the outset of this project.

*For My Lovely Wife*
*Kristine Ellen*
*The Love of My Life*
*And Also For My Beautiful Daughter*
*Erika Kristine*
*And For My Newborn Granddaughter*
*Ava Kristine*
*Who Both Will Carry Her Namesake Forward*

# PROLOGUE

This account is intended to be autobiographical, yet not necessarily personal. There will of necessity be a personal timeline since one cannot describe a home without discussing the specifics of the material and work that first went into making it a house. But an attempt will be made to discuss these personal milestones in the milieu of the events that preceded, coexisted and shaped this life of mine.

What is there about this subject that warrants the time and effort to write it and even more for someone to read it? Let me answer this query first by referring to the latter part of the title, namely the times in which I have lived. Much has been written and continues to be written about our modern times. There is no question that this period is important and well worth the effort to write about it and for another to read what may be written. It is hoped that my own perspective will add something unique to the mix of voices heard.

The twentieth century has been, to paraphrase Dickens, "the best of times and the worst of times", using almost any yardstick to measure. It has been a time of unparalleled progress in science and technology. In 1900 a man could expect an average lifespan of 46 years but by the year 2000 that almost doubled to 74 years[1]. The ability to harness energy from oil, coal, and now nuclear sources is beyond the imagination of those who lived in the nineteenth century, much less those who lived before. The freedom of many to enjoy leisure time has never been greater as inventions have taken much of the drudgery away that used to consume much of our day.

But at the same time, the twentieth century has been by far the most brutal and bloody of all recorded history, and human history has recorded many previous horrors. There is no other period that has the sheer magnitude of carnage as that under discussion. The technological achievements that led to greater human happiness have also made the depredations of evil mass murderers and their state run organizations more deadly than the world has ever known. The inventions that helped modern man to enjoy life have been usurped by madmen to operate armies, death camps and surveillance systems which have been used to enslave their neighbors and much more often their own countrymen. As many as 125 million poor souls have prematurely met their end in the twentieth century[2] at the hands of such men as Wilhelm II, Lenin, Stalin, Mussolini, Hitler, Hirohito, Mao, Pol Pot and others. This startling number gives us sober reflection on the unchanging nature of mankind over time. Under the patina of civilization that we have been able to develop there is the Manichaean fact that the dark side of mankind is always present.

As we move into the twenty-first century there is no indication of substantial change in this pattern. The findings of the Hubble telescope relative to our galaxy and the developments of magnetic and computerized imaging of the human body are juxtaposed with the suicidal attack on the twin towers resulting in the deaths of thousands of innocents. The stunning achievements of the twenty-first century mind are contrasted by the insane actions of radical Islamists with a seventh century mind-set. Hamlet's soliloquy on our nature . . . "What a piece of work is a man! How noble in reason! How infinite in faculty!"[3] . . . is contrasted by the Hobbesian caricature of an Osama Bin Laden. These are the times in which I have lived and continue to function. This is the stage and action of the greater play in which I have been but a minor player.

Humility would suggest that a bit player may have little edifying to say about himself in relation to these larger forces we have seen. Most bit players do not write about themselves and like those "rude forefathers of the hamlet" in Gray's *Elegy*[4] let the epitaph on the gravestone speak their legacy. Admittedly, like historians as various as Herodotus and Winston Churchill, I subscribe to the dictum that history is not made from vague social forces moving societies one way or the other. It is a product of the actions of specific men and women confronting the situations of their day using whatever free will that the Almighty gives them. This implies that great individuals making choices for good or evil determine the course of events.

Where does a bit player fit into this? I have not been an appointed head of state, an officer in great armies nor have I been an innovator of novel things in my chosen field of medicine. In fact, I have never held public office, have not even been a member of the armed services and have not won high distinction in medicine. Furthermore, it might be said that even those around me as family and friends have only occasionally and tangentially had contact with the prime and secondary players of our day.

Thus what would a reader gain from these musings that would repay his effort. As the current of the twentieth century moves inexorably into the twenty-first, of what value is this sidebar? As the great river of our history flows mightily through the rapids consider that there may be something to be learned from the study of the pools and eddies on its shallow sides. Perhaps from the particulars of these pools might come some insights to the parallel flow of the mainstream as we proceed along our way. Although the greater actions are taken in the limelight of history and unquestionably these have direct effects on the lesser actors, it is just as likely that the actions of the lesser actors in turn magnify and redefine the primary players. That we all have some consequence in history whether great or small seems in keeping with our ideals of God given individual worth and responsibility and is not merely a sop to the credulous. If man is made in God's image, does he not have something valuable to say? What from each individual is truthful and what is not? The answers must be carefully sought. To find wisdom in this river of history is to define the magnitude and direction of the cross currents between the rapids and the pools. It is in this light that the present writing is offered and in this hope that it will be read.

There is some value to speak of my perspective before examining this life and others that may be mentioned herein. In this therapeutic age in which we live there is no intent herein to write another self help treatise. There is no question that certain things that I have done and certain roads that I have taken are incorrect as seen from the standpoint of later experience and knowledge. Yet there should be no sense of regret in this regard for none is intended. I feel that whatever else life is, it is a great gift from our maker. He has set us on a journey and has given us some amount of free choice in how we travel. He does not expect perfection but demands effort.

If we take a road on that journey that is not right for us and others, it is our obligation to reclaim our way and attempt to correct our course. It can only be determined what is right by giving our effort to the direction we have taken and by measuring our progress against our natural sense of right and wrong and what we learn of the lessons imparted to us by our forebears. Since human wisdom is imperfect and comes only from experience and study over time, it follows that we cannot be correct in all our choices early on, if in fact ever. With the passage of time and with God's blessing our odds of making a proper choice will hopefully improve. In approaching life in this way we avoid the pitfalls of negativity and regret and their offspring of victim-hood and jealousy. In righting a wrong course of travel it seems that a positive approach of greater effort in the correct direction beats the paralysis of humiliation and self pity any day, any time. With these ground rules the story will proceed. An attempt will be made to place the life of this bit player in the greater waters of his times whenever possible. We will start with my parents and their generation, those who preceded my own timeline and brought me forth. In chronological fashion will ensue youth and family life, education, courtship and marriage, medical training and practice. The changes entailed and the excitement of raising a family of my own and the pleasure of the growth and maturation of children will follow. Family, friends and acquaintances will weave their way in and out of this narrative. We will proceed (without regret) to the world of the stormy present and (with trepidation) measure its portents for the future. It is my hope that in this way I can successfully answer the question of "why" posed above.

# CHAPTER 1

## PARENTS OF THE BABY BOOM

W hen he returned from his service in the U.S. Air Force Ray Leonard was a shaken man. After 35 missions over occupied France and enemy Germany as a waist gunner on a B24 Liberator, Staff Sgt. R.B. Leonard welcomed his leave from the 713th Bomb Squadron of the 448th Heavy of the Eighth Air Force. He received the Air Medal with its five oak leaf clusters and was sent home to Aurora, Indiana on furlough.

However, his experience at an air station near Upminster, England came at a price. All his life he had been afraid of heights. As a kid on a trip to Washington, D.C. he had to crawl backwards down the stairway of the Washington Monument and, on another occasion, was terrified into almost jumping in panic from a Ferris wheel ride at an amusement park. The stress of waiting around the air base for his crew's next flight orders was in itself enough of an ordeal, since the bar of how many missions were needed to complete their service was constantly raised during the war. But the actual missions, which took place in daylight at an average altitude of 23,000 feet and in an unpressurized plane at temperatures averaging -30 degrees F. required superlative mental effort for this air- scared recruit. The flak was often intense and all around the planes, and the statistics of how many of these crews were lost during these missions was a shadow that followed these men on every flight[5] . Standing at the waist of the bomber with the wind whistling around him and held by a strap to the thin skeleton of the craft was especially hard for Sgt. Leonard who would not take an amusement ride for the rest of his life. Was he glad when the 35th and final mission was completed? His entry into his flight diary should suffice on this point. The last lines record "Time to call it my day. Finis . . . . That's all brother!"

Returning to his home town in southern Indiana, he married his high school sweetheart, Emma Pearle Randall, at her family home on Route 50. Her father Clyde Randall was not happy about the marriage because he knew of the likelihood that this soldier husband might not make it home to his bride from further service in the war. These fly boys of the USAF still might be needed in the war in the pacific, even though furloughed from service in Europe. Nevertheless, Emma's father consented and the wedding took place on March 31, 1945. The newlyweds drove to Chicago for a reception at the Graemore Hotel with Ray's side of the family. They then took a train to Miami where the Army provided a hotel for airmen on leave and for this couple a honeymoon respite[6].

The wedding and honeymoon was not idyllic, however, since Ray was suffering from battle fatigue. It has been called shell shock, soldier's heart, and in our own therapeutic age, it is labeled post traumatic stress disorder (PTSD). Whatever you call it, it has probably been around since men have gone to war. Ray and Emma were convinced that after the break in Miami his orders would require him to fly over enemy Japan They were equally convinced that if that happened, his number would be up. Everyone knew how bloody the battle in the Pacific had been. The predictions of the military minds for the toll of American dead in the coming battle of the Japanese mainland were as much as one million. This estimate was based on the suicidal terrorism displayed by Japanese troops and citizens during the horrific battles of Iwo Jima and Okinawa late in the war. None of this bode well for the future of these newly-marrieds as they sat on the beaches of the resort town in Florida in 1945. According to plan, Ray would report back to camp Atterbury soon.

It was a literal God-send when Harry Truman decided to use the nuclear bomb, and when in the aftermath of Hiroshima and Nagasaki the Japanese finally capitulated. For Americans involved with that war, and at that time, there was no other choice to be made[7]. Imperial Japan had demonstrated time and again that only such measures would shake their determination to sacrifice to the last man and woman in their war effort. It was the bomb that saved Ray from the inferno and many at that time felt the same about themselves. Later generations, less familiar with the full history of those times and much more relativistic in their judgments, have decried the brutality of the use of those nuclear bombs. From a safe vantage point of time and born of the subsequent cold war standoff, some of the present day critics of those American decision makers have formulated a much different scenario of (non) action.

The end of the war erased the demons from Ray's mind and it was not long after military discharge that he went back to school. On the GI Bill, Ray finished his business degree at Indiana University. Bloomington was a smaller, sleepier town then than it is now as a Big Ten member and mega-university, but it was an exciting time for the returning soldier and his new bride. They rented an apartment at 319 N. Washington and went to work and study. Emma became pregnant and their first child Stephen Raymond was born less than one year later on April 2nd. Graduation in 1948 was time to look for work and a number of starter jobs ensued as necessity called to support the young family.

It was a good time to be alive for the World War II generation. Many did not make it back and the many that did were scarred from their time in the trenches. But most of those fortunate enough to live set about to solve the less dire problems of making ends meet. The great economic engine of the U.S. economy that had stalled during the depression years roared back during the war years as the "arsenal of democracy" supplied material to all the allies in order to clinch victory. At war's end the same generous nation sent even more men and materiel to rebuild the shattered nations of not only our friends but also our former enemies[8]. There was much work to be done and the unified spirit that had taken the nation through the dark days of the war turned to a general optimism afterwards. It was an optimism born of the reality that the twin scourges of depression and war were past and it was not daunted by the new reality of Soviet imperialism and the mutually assured destruction of nuclear standoff.

The wartime interlude of battle fatigue was not in keeping with Ray's general approach to life and with the war over he returned to the positive side. Optimism came almost constitutionally to Ray Leonard. Not only did he give thanks to his Maker to be alive, it was built into his genes to be upbeat.

Keeping upbeat might have been learned best in the prewar years of the depression and was an outlook that both Ray and Emma shared, but likely for different reasons. The Randall family had weathered the depression without the stigma of soup lines and dispossession that had afflicted the Ralph and Bertha Leonard family. Clyde Randall was a successful farmer, a past member of the county council, a township trustee and a director of the First National Bank of Aurora. He was a good father and generous patriarch of his farm. Clyde's wife, born Jeanette Pearle Miller, graduated from Moores Hill College[9] in 1907. It was unusual at that time for a woman to become a college graduate. She taught school and married in 1909. She was an expert gardener and cook for her family of six sons and three daughters.

During the depression years, Clyde and Jeanette Pearle (everyone called her Pearle) would frequently feed the destitute families that rolled up U.S. Route 50 in wagons with their kids and possessions piled high. There was always enough food to go around to the nine Randall kids and some left over to offer to those highway travelers who had none. It was a curiosity that the recipients of the Randall largesse would frequently eat and leave without even saying thanks. Maybe it was pride, maybe it was shame, maybe it was both. Whatever it was, it always stuck in Emma's mind that people have a hard time being indebted to the generosity of others. On a larger scale, it is tempting to draw a parallel to the attitude of the French in our time. After American blood and treasure was spent to defend their land from the German invasion of WWI and from the Nazis in WWII, they now denigrate and oppose us at every turn[10].

As for the effects of the collapsing economy on the Randall family, it was not good for produce prices and it made it much less likely that the girls could order a new dress through the Sears and Roebuck catalogue. But with hard work around the farm there was always enough food and thus everybody held together. That may be one reason for Emma's optimism; however, the failing health of her mother Pearle tempered her outlook. Pearle developed high blood pressure and there was, unfortunately, little treatment for hypertension in those years. After several strokes she died in December, 1941, at the age of 58. Emma was only nineteen at that time. Losing her was a tragedy for the whole family, but it was typical of those times that there was little effective treatment for a common condition like hypertension.

FDR himself succumbed to the same malady before WW II drew to a close[11]. Only a few decades later the medical and pharmaceutical discoveries would make a host of effective treatments available to the public for these conditions. We can only speculate what turns history would have taken if later technological discoveries would have happened earlier, but that is the Pandora's Box of historical succession that is better left closed.

Ray's father, Ralph Leonard, was out of work in Chicago in the early 1930's, so his family needed whatever assistance they could get. Ralph was the conduit for the upbeat genes that Ray received. He had a penchant for drama and farce that was to be a real treat for his future grandchildren. There were rumors in the family that his real mother was an actress on the silent screen. He was a veteran of WWI and he had a life-long love of cars, even during the depression, when he could not afford one. After the war he was, able to purchase a Hudson. He cherished that car and drove it with abandon until he contracted cancer and died in 1958.

Ray's mother, a slim, pretty German fraulein with the maiden name of Bertha Carolina Wilhelmina Heise was a flinty match for Ralph. He used to say that "you should watch out for those skinny women because they can give you splinters!" During the depression, "Birdy" as she was called, once sent her son Ray to a birthday party for a friend without a present because the family actually could not afford one. This so-called friend would not let Ray into the party and the humiliation of that episode became an indelible mark on his consciousness. He never blamed his mother, of course, but he determined that he would make himself a good provider for those around him from there on. Ray always had jobs when he was young and he was a firm believer that work was essential for a young person's character. He put that belief into action with his own children later on.

At the age of nine, Ray composed a letter to President Roosevelt, telling him that his father was a good man and asking the president to please find him a job. Whether that letter had something to do with Ralph's subsequent hiring as a federal treasury agent is not certain but the other members of the family are convinced that it did. That job required agent Leonard to provide oversight at several liquor distilleries, so the family moved to Wisconsin, Washington, D.C., and finally to Aurora, Indiana. There Ralph was assigned to the Seagrams and Schenley plants in Lawrenceberg, Indiana.

It was in Aurora that Ray and his sister Lorraine attended school and where he met his future wife Emma. Ray's part time jobs while attending school were not just for spending money but also for contributing to the family expenses. Because of these jobs he could not participate in many extracurricular activities and was on the track team only once. Since Ray was originally from Chicago, some in that small town in Southern Indiana saw him as a "city slicker". Even some of Emma's older brothers teased him about that. All said, the glass was always half full to Ray Leonard and those upbeat genes were undaunted in Aurora and afterward.

By 1948, with a college diploma in hand and with the first-born son now two, Ray and Emma moved to Muncie, Indiana where Ray was hired b y Owens-Illinois Glass Company. In September of that year my brother, Clyde Ralph Leonard, was born, having the given names of both of his grandfathers. When he was laid off from Owens, Ray then interviewed with and was hired by Ford Motor Company. Subsequently, there were several moves around the Detroit area while a new home was built in West Dearborn on Hollander Sreet. Emma became pregnant again and at the old Women's Hospital in Detroit, she delivered her third son, Mark William Leonard. Women's Hospital later changed its name to Hutzel Hospital as part of the Wayne Medical School. This was where I later took my medical school obstetrics rotation and it also became site of two of my own children's births. But that is a story we will yet recount.

The three boys, Steve, Clyde and Mark, each born two years apart, would be the "first" family of Ray and Emma Leonard. We boys did many things together and became great buddies, although I always had the envious position of greater age and size on the other two—at least until much later. In future years we often teased our younger sister and brother that the "second" Leonard family was only a mistaken parental afterthought.

Life in Dearborn was good. One might say from the Leonard family's standpoint it was very good. Dearborn was a bustling place in the 1950's. It was the home of Ford Motor Company and that provided a substantial tax base for public benefits. There was a never ending supply of parks to play in and twenty-six public swimming pools for those who were residents of the city. Levagood Park with its swimming pool called Seashore was our favorite place to go in the summer months. Getting there required my mom to accompany me across busy Telegraph Road until I was older and could be trusted to get there on my own. Howard Elementary School, which we attended, was just down the block and only a short run or fast bike ride away. The spacious park around the school had baseball fields, swings and slides, and enough trees where night time games of capture the flag went on with almost military seriousness. It was important for a young kid to find out that there was a pecking order in the neighborhood and that the older kids would enforce order on younger ones that stepped out of line. I adapted to the rough and tumble rules and fit in.

The homes in West Dearborn were neat and well-kept; each had a garage and a small yard that was usually well-trimmed. They had the appearance of sameness which led social critics of the 1950's to imply that they produced an identical sort of dull and unexciting people. Superficially, these neighborhoods probably did in fact look fairly uniform. These were the homes of the supposedly boring "Ozzie and Harriet" generation. Condescendingly, Pete Seeger, a folklorist and political activist singer, sang a song called "Little Boxes" in which he deplored the "Little boxes made of ticky tacky . . . they all look the same"[12].

Because Dearborn was a "white" city and also because its overtly racist mayor pledged to keep blacks out of his town[13], it was easy for some to conclude that its residents were predictably bigoted and racist, in addition to their shortcomings of cultural uniformity. However, this is a great over simplification. The majority of these people were hard working and many were back from the same war, a war that spread them over the globe in various states of danger and deprivation. After what they had seen they wanted a "good" life and "good" things for their families. They took pride in ownership of their homes, however look-alike they might appear to some. Their kids were rough and sometimes even raucous. To be sure, many caught on to trends glorified in the popular culture such as the renegade, cigarette smoking, blue suede shoes, tough-guy images they saw. Yet, if the truth were known, the families in those neighborhoods probably had more "diversity" (to use a later term) of thought and experience than is known today in many more visually diverse neighborhoods.

Dearborn in the 1950's was a great place for a young boy to get his legs about himself. Some of my friends were on the unrestrained side and I learned to be a bit of the same, albeit within the long arm of the house rules of Ray Leonard. Gary C. could get away with just about anything because his dad and mom were arguing so much that they did not always notice him.

Chuckie P. lived across the street and always told us that his well endowed and good-looking mother ironed the family's clothes in the nude. None of us ever saw that spectacle but we could imagine it and the thought would titillate us as only young boys could be. Jerry K. was incorrigible in school where I helped him misbehave, but incredulously to me, he was the same at home. I knew that I could get away with smart-ass behavior in the elementary school because the worst punishment was to be sent out in the hallway or ordered to sit in the girl's bathroom. More severe infractions could earn me a trip to Mr. Wilson's room where he would administer a whack on the backside with his aerated wooden ruler. But I could not fathom the same behavior at home because when Ray Leonard came home from Ford Motor Company, my mother's report would result in discipline worse than Mr. Wilson could ever deliver.

Just so there is no misinformation about my cultural education, I will posit right here that I walked home for lunch almost every day from Howard School and had lunch with Soupy Sales. I ate a peanut butter and jelly sandwich while he cavorted around the set cracking jokes that only a kid would like and took a few cream pies in the face for good measure. I could imitate White Fang and Black Tooth, take the "good bird bath pledge" and, if I was really lucky, I could talk my parents into letting me stay up for his grown-up show at night. The Soupy Shuffle was the first dance that I ever learned. It was also the only step I knew until I learned The Bop, which I practiced in my baseball cleats on the baseball diamond over at Howard Field. By the fourth grade I picked up a few other moves and even went over to Betty F's house and practiced with her in the basement. We could really rock to those 45's and I have loved dancing ever since.

It was a great time to be alive for the Leonard family. Dad was getting promotions at Ford; Clyde, Mark and I had many interesting places to play. Best of all, we had a Mom who was always home for her kids. Dad would throw the ball with us in the backyard, and on weekends he would even let us have a sip of his beer when the neighbors came over to sit and talk in the driveway. On leap year of 1956, Mom went to Oakwood hospital to give birth to my sister Kimberly Anne. Since I was ten years old, I was allowed to help my mom with the new baby's care. I can still remember singing "Down in the Valley" to her as I changed her diaper that first summer after she was born. We were sitting on the folding chairs in the backyard and the sun was warm on us, there at 23737 Hollander.

# CHAPTER 2

## THE YOUNG FAMILY MOVES

D ad did well at Ford Motor Company. He was promoted to supervisor of labor relations and personnel services. His responsibilities included union and management-labor negotiations. This position came with considerable stress, so cigarettes were a useful stress reliever. Actually, he had smoked since he was a youngster, but during the war his smoking increased considerably. The minute those Liberators touched down the crew could not wait to get to terra firma and light one up. Cigarettes were cheap at the military PX so they were an inexpensive friend to the airmen as they anxiously awaited their next mission. During the long contract negotiations at Ford Motor Company, Dad found that cigarettes were a similar comfort.

When talks failed there were occasional labor strikes. In his supervisory position, Dad had to go into work during these strikes. Union picketers blocked the gates of the plant and used verbal and physical intimidation to stop the managers from entering. These union men did not feel too considerate of the needs of the salaried employees to keep things going during the strike so the company might survive. Being a loyal company man and thankful to have his job, Ray Leonard could not fathom the attitude that he saw. To strike or picket a job that the company offered was not in his mind set, even if there were some things that could not be agreed on. It also rankled him that many striking employees who bought bread for their families with wages earned at Ford Motor Company would actually purchase other makes of cars which they shamelessly parked in the Ford parking lot. These labor disputes deeply irritated him, because he sensed no similar sense of loyalty across the table.

I could never understand at the time why Dad reacted so vehemently to the popular song "Sixteen Tons" by Tennessee Ernie Ford. To me it had a good beat and easy words. The chorus line proceeds "you load sixteen tons and whatya' get, another day older and deeper in debt, Saint Peter don't call me 'cause I can't go, I owe my soul to the company's toll". One time when I sang those words at home, it really brought out a father's Philippic. "Those poor dears", he retorted sharply, "too bad that they have a job with that company and are actually required to work!" I did not understand at the time, but the essence of his response was that he was tired of hearing moaning and complaining from men who had good jobs and benefits for which many others would give their right arm. He was not about to listen to more whining from some popular song, no matter who sang it. Ray was a member of the party of Lincoln and like Lincoln he believed in a man's right to rise through his own labor[14]. Wage labor was the way that men could better themselves and their families. No job was too menial if it put food on the table. It was the American way. It was Ray Leonard's way.

And rise he did. After a few promotions Ray and Emma were in a financial position to consider moving to a new home, one with more space to meet the needs of the growing family. I did not care much for this idea. In fact, I would have much preferred a tonsillectomy, even though I really did not know what that entailed at the time. It seemed to me that the home we had was just fine. Furthermore, for a kid just about to enter the fifth grade there was no need to move away from all those good friends I had and a neighborhood that suited me well. Nevertheless, the "die was cast", and with Caesar we crossed the Rubicon and left Dearborn behind. Our new home was in the suburb of Grosse Ile, which was downriver from Detroit. My younger brothers and sister greeted this change with the excitement and anticipation of a new place. However, I had a hard adjustment to that move. To begin with, Grosse Ile was a very different place than Dearborn. The early French explorers of the 18th century named this island that was situated in the Detroit River *la grosse ile* (the large island). The southern tip of the island jutted out into Lake Erie and Amherstburg, Canada was just across the east river side. In 1776 it was sold to several Detroit merchants by the Pottawatomie Indians and by the 1950's the only Francophile remnant that remained was the spelling of its name. Grosse Ile had been largely residential and not commercial for most of its history, although a Naval Air Base was constructed on its southern tip in WW II.

At the time of our move, Grosse Ile consisted mainly of middle class homes, but there were magnificent upper class homes as well. Many of the latter were located along the river with rolling lawns and gardens around them. These residents were distinguished by "old wealth" as opposed to the "new wealth" of those residents recently transplanted to subdivisions there. There were country clubs with golfing and swimming activities. There were boat and yacht clubs for those who owned watercraft that buzzed up and down the Detroit River.

The whole place had a totally different feel from the busy closeness of the neighborhoods of West Dearborn off of Telegraph Road. The community was much more spread out and kids did not congregate on the streets as much. I would, over time, come to like the semi-rural, small town feel of "the island", as its residents called it, but back then what I saw struck me as physically foreign and socially remote.

Initially I had the impression that it was going to be difficult to make new friends. That perception was only magnified when I became the new student in Mrs. Wallbridge's 5th grade classroom. Feeling defensive about myself, and feeling isolated from the in-crowd, I did what I had learned in Dearborn. I fought. I picked so many fights at recess that I ended up spending a good deal of that first year in the office of the principal, Mr. Roher. This was not any worse than the girl's bathroom at Howard elementary, so my main focus was to act as if the detention did not bother me.

In retrospect, Mrs. Wallbridge was a good lady and did not deserve my behavior. On one occasion, when I showed up with a "ducktail and waterfall" hairdo in her classroom, she wisely sent me back to the bathroom to re-comb my hair. Back then, this was an embarrassing moment; but I now thank her for helping me to be accepted by my new peers. It took several years for me to get over the rebel image I tried to create in order to cover up my feelings of insecurity. Ultimately, with the steady hand of a mother at home who gave me good advice and with a father who set standards of behavior, I successfully made the transition to my new hometown.

Sports played a part in rescuing me from my antisocial behavior, just as it continues to do for young people today. I enjoyed competition of any kind and especially liked baseball, football and basketball. In baseball, there were organized games of "Little League". The difference back then was that kids showed up and played in a much more unstructured way than they do today. It was good for the kids to work out their play and their differences much more on their own with a minimum of adult interference. The current generations of kids have so many coaches, assistant coaches, player drafts, required practices, travel schedules and parents in the stands that one would think that it was the major league rather than little league. Coaches today sometimes complain that their players lack the ability to improvise when a new situation arises on the court or field that they may not have seen in practice. Perhaps the highly structured condition of our current sports programs is to blame. Kids that play more pick up games are used to improvising and are not befuddled by an unusual game situation.

I also have to credit work for some of my redemption from the "James Dean" persona that I brought with me to my new environs. In fact, if James Dean had a job to go to, maybe he would not have been standing around next to that motorcycle pouting in his state of ennui. The structure of having a job to do and work at home to complete also contributed to my eventual maturation.

Even before our move to Grosse Ile, I sold The Detroit Free Press on the busy corners of Ford Rd. and Cherry Hill where they intersected Telegraph Rd. in Dearborn. Regularly, Dad would get me up at 5 AM and take me down to the corners where he sat and read the morning news while I hustled the papers to the commuters waiting at the stop lights. I had a belt coin-changer and learned to make quick change between the lanes of traffic before the light turned and the cars roared on. I kept my earnings confined to a cigar box and at the end of each week I tallied up what was left after disbursements to my supplier. I can remember the great feeling when there was often up to $10 in that cigar box at the end of the week. This was a king's wage to a ten year old!

After moving to Grosse Ile, I acquired a paper route which wound around the subdivisions near our home at 7934 Coventry. I delivered those papers on my Schwinn Huffy come rain, sleet or snow. Here, I learned a lesson from my customers, especially if the paper was missed, not folded properly, or ended up in the bushes. A satisfied customer meant a tip now and then, but a disgruntled one was a real headache upon the next encounter. This kept the incipient paperboy's attention focused on the details and it was like having a whole bunch of fathers along my route.

Over time, I realized that it was not fair that I had initially prejudged the folks in my new home town. Sure, there were many that were very affluent compared to the modest lifestyle of our own family. There were also many that were on an economic par with us as well as many below that mark. Moreover, what did that have to do with what kind of people they were? If a few were stuffed shirts why did that have to reflect on the rest? In spite of the clothes they wore and the club memberships they had, many of the more affluent families were hard working and upwardly mobile just like the Ray Leonard's were. Those below our place in this mix were often trying to improve their status. There were some who seemed to inherit wealth but how could one know what it took to maintain what they had. There were very few that appeared to live an idealized life of leisure, and if so, so what!

What I did was to make a childish conclusion to what I

superficially noticed. Dearborn had a tough guy, blue collar kind of image. Grosse Ile had a more refined, white collar image. In a child's mind appearances can be transposed into reality since the child does not understand the complexity that time weaves into the person. A child assumes that if two people look different, then they probably are and acts accordingly. I made my own assumptions and ended up in the principal's office. I would not understand for some time, in fact many years, that people in these United States generally play by the same basic rules. Whether they live in a suburb or in the country, whether they reside in the North, South, East or West, they are under a system of law and an economic necessity to earn a living. They work harder and are remunerated more fairly here than in any other place in the earth. Our system is not always fair but it is as close as men have come to a meritocracy in history. Those wealthy people living in large homes on East River Drive were not landed barons living in South America or princes from oil rich Saudi Arabia. There should not be some moral equivalence made as if wealth is wealth the world over. Someone should not assume something about them as if they came by their wealth by robbing the poor and cheating the middle class. It took longer than I want to admit for these insights to really sink in, but once it did, it simplified things. Instead of being jealous or resentful of the position of others, it is much more useful to wish them well and concentrate on what you yourself need to do to find happiness. The commandment not to covet is, in my opinion, the most frequently broken of the Decalogue.

All of this brings the discussion back to the child's mind. What I did then was childish, but then at age eleven I was a child. What passes for adult debate in the popular and political culture having to do with class warfare is equally childish. It amounts to no more than jealousy from one group (i.e.-blue collar) to another (i.e.-white collar). Every time something reasonable for the public is proposed, such as tax cuts or social security savings accounts, the (childish) refrain is that these are tax cuts and savings accounts for the rich. Every time the salary of an entrepreneur, a CEO, an entertainer or an athlete is reported there is the inevitable refrain that they are paid "too much". It is as if the genius making that claim could devise a better system of pay than the market has done[15]. Just as I reacted out of insecurity and used the only hold on power I knew, so the demagogues continue to poison the public well with such harangues.

Over time, I began to feel more comfortable in our new home town. I made some new friends and still had my brothers and sister for play. The Leonard kids had a good life on Grosse Ile. There were woods to explore nearby and the river for play in the summer and skating in the winter. There was a good-sized back yard, much larger than in Dearborn and the Catholic elementary school play yard just a few blocks away. Our mother was always at home for her kids through these years. She became pregnant and then delivered her fourth son at Wyandotte General Hospital on August 15, 1959, Raymond B. Leonard II. There were thirteen years between the first and last of her children.

Little by little my bellicosity at school waned. There were less detentions and my behavior, although not exemplary, improved in class. It took some years before it sank in that doing well in school academically was more important for my future than I expected and not just some feigned performance of an obsequious student. This lesson slowly wended its way into my consciousness as my high school years approached and I considered what kind of future I envisioned. A key thing that I discovered was that with some application of effort I could actually do well in the classroom. I owe much to my teachers that they helped to prove this proposition to me.

Not insignificant is the part played by my parents. Dad had a penchant for speaking and writing and this rubbed off on me. Moreover, Mom was a well educated woman, who although lacking a college education did well in her high school years. She was a reader of books for pleasure and always read to us kids. It was a revelation to me that her interest in reading and biblical study over time stirred in me some of the same interests. In our later years, this has become a warm mutual connection and something that we share, in spite of the distance that separates us.

# CHAPTER 3

## HIGH SCHOOL IN THE 1960'S

In only a few years following the family's move to Grosse Ile it was time for me to enter high school and the 9th grade. As anyone who has been back to their high school reunions can attest, high school experiences are not the same for everyone. Not present are those who, although living in the same town, religiously avoid these affairs. Also not accounted for are those who moved away and never kept in touch with any of their classmates. Even when efforts are made by reunion planners to locate them, they can never be found. One can only conclude that, unlike their other classmates, they do not want to revisit that time in their lives. Obviously, the high school years were not as memorable for some as they were for others.

Inevitably, the dynamic that underlies this phenomenon is whether the individual felt accepted into the mainstream of the peer group or not. Although group identification or rejection is probably an oversimplification of the situation, in almost any generation it has some validity as an explanation. In every society there is a dominant culture and a counter culture. In the 1950's, there were "beatniks" and "hoods" that were juxtaposed to the "straights" and "preppies". James Dean was the counterpart of Annette Funicello. In the 1960's there were "hippies" and "yippies", "preppies" and "nerds".

The mainstream cultural influence for teenagers in the 60's included traditional rock and roll rock music, the British invasion of The Beatles and the Motown sound from the city of Detroit. This was piped in to the homes of viewers via television's Ed Sullivan Show and Dick Clark's American Bandstand. The venue of the rock concert also gained in popularity. Musical taste could sometimes contribute to the dividing lines in the youth culture at even the high school level.

In a similar fashion, athletic participation was a source of either identification with the larger group or isolation from it. Athletic competition has always been a popular American past time, but in the 1960's there was a burgeoning of big time high school and college programs that could further divide the student body. The "jocks" became more of an isolated in-group in which others did not feel, or care to feel, included. It is not that these divisions began in the 60's, but that they progressed in magnitude during that decade. The continuum for these tendencies is still in operation.

As I entered Grosse Ile High School in 1960, these influences in the culture were part of my milieu. I came to my new community at the elementary level and was a decided outsider. However, over time my interests and tastes became similar to the majority of my classmates. I no longer felt estranged from the activities in school and participated fully in them. In retrospect, my four years in high school were a positive experience for me, I have good recollections of them, and have attended most of the reunions that the class of 64 has had. Of course, there are things that I now realize were conceived incompletely or even badly but that is part of growing up. While there is no effort of a *mea culpa* here, it is important to examine the period of this decade and its influence on me further.

The decade of the 1960's has been written and talked about in great detail. For many, it still represents a time of tumultuous change for the better in American society. Part of our society saw it then, and many see it now, as if it represented a "great awakening" of secular America just as the first three great awakenings of prior centuries represented landmarks for the religious life of this country[16]. Their reflections on this time emphasize the progress toward racial tolerance represented by Martin Luther King's sit-ins and protests in Selma, Alabama. They touted the passage of the Civil Rights Law of 1964 that wiped out Jim Crow and made official racism illegal. They were proud of the public protest against the Vietnam War and their part in changing the course of American commitment to that part of Asia. They look back longingly at the fresh look in public life represented by President John Kennedy and his entourage who created "Camelot" in the governing class. They were equally proud of the loosening of the stifling strictures they perceived in traditional American morality and applauded the student protests and community revolts that changed society for the better as they saw it.

Those persuaded by the beneficial effects of that decade of momentous change focus on only part of the story. Their opinion is not daunted by the metamorphosis of civil rights into black separatism and affirmative action in the years following King's assassination. Nor are they persuaded from the logic of the peace movement by the subsequent carnage and loss of stature by an American abandonment of its own commitments in Vietnam and Southeast Asia. The aura of Camelot persists in the minds Kennedy supporters in spite of the subsequent revelations of how close we came to nuclear war in Cuba, how he really lost to Khrushchev in the process[17], how he escalated the commitment to South Vietnam while engineering a *coup* that left our ally Diem dead and how JFK had numerous secret affairs with mistresses while Jackie played hostess to the national psyche at the White House[18].

The student unrest of this period and its charge that education had to be "relevant" has arguably paved the way for the decline of academic standards, resulting in an erosion of SAT scores and other measures of real learning[19]. Furthermore, the concurrent attack on traditional moral values and the status of the nuclear family ushered in a moral relativism that leaves present day youth unable to make moral judgments about important issues. Without question, this has contributed to the soaring rate of single parent families and an increase in juvenile delinquency.

Here, within these two decades, are the beginnings of the cultural divide which we in the present day call the "culture wars". There have always been factions of opinion in our land. Our Constitutional Framers warned us of that and some space is devoted to that subject in *The Federalist*[20]. Certainly, our current differences are not on a scale with the magnitude of enmity present at the time of the Civil War when outright military action left 620,000 dead in its wake[21]. However, the present situation is clearly different from many other periods in our history. There is, for instance, a clear break from the unity that the nation exhibited during the time of the Second World War.

In this context there is a great distinction from what went before the era of the 1960's. The political and cultural tensions existing in the decade of the 1950's took a huge leap forward during the next decade. These opposing worldviews have become virtually irrevocable in their present day manifestation. The election of 2000 is a good foil for the more recent battle lines of these wars. The results of the voting in the contest of Bush vs. Gore were so close that the ultimate decision involved the attention of the Supreme Court and the outcome of its deliberation is still considered illegitimate by many on the Democrat left. Furthermore, as we listen to the current debate over our involvement in the post September 11th war on terror, the sides have become shriller by the month and the partisans do not seem to agree even on the ground rules of discourse.

It is of interest to look at the influence of the mainstream media on the course of the divide that is seen. Here again, there is no general agreement from the sparring sides as to that influence. Using once more the Civil War as a reference point, it is found that at that time there was no pretension of objectivity from the press. During the Lincoln-Douglas debates, papers favorable to Lincoln and the Republicans would write frankly glowing reports of Lincoln's speeches and utterly damning reports of those of Douglas. The papers favorable to Douglas and the

Democrats would do just the opposite. These papers often were so partisan that they would print copies of the speeches that were overtly altered and not at all reflecting what was actually said. The savvy citizen would thus read both accounts and piece together the truth of the matter for himself.

It is counterintuitive that anyone in the press could completely ignore subjectivity in their reporting so the savvy citizen of today should again read widely in order to ferret out the truth of their reports. The major print and network media of the latter 20th century have convinced themselves that they do not suffer from the sort of bias manifested by their 19th century counterparts. They have posited the shibboleth of objectivity and acclaim it in their newsrooms, as in their journalism schools. The media's belief in this chimera began in the decade of the 60's and it has been elevated to a Holy Grail in our present day. As with anything sacred, even the suggestion that things are not what is claimed, brings not a reasoned response but a raft of fervent denials that implies blasphemy on the part of the questioner[22].

Looking back to the media treatment of the 1960 presidential election with the benefit of later historical knowledge, some interesting things appear that might not have been obvious then. Big media at the time was print media, and just as the New York Times dominates today, so they did then. There were, of course, other papers in the Washington, Boston and New York area but politicians knew that they had to have favorable treatment by the Eastern establishment to run a successful campaign. It was also the time of the rise of the influence of television in the political process and this proved to be a powerful force for the one side or the other.

Even then it was clear that the media conglomerate showed favoritism with their reporting. They tolerated Eisenhower because he had such a loyal following in the public. They portrayed him as a nice old man who liked to play golf but who was not as bright as someone like Adlai Stevenson, who was considered by the media to be a "thinker". However, Ike, the wily old fox, had arranged that image fairly purposely as the recent release of his phone logs and diaries attest[23]. This former Supreme Allied Commander, on whose watch the Second War was won, allowed the press and the public to think he was playing golf while he secretly called around the world each day to his command posts to contain the Soviet threat in the deadly serious cold war. Running the Washington political apparatus was not as hard as taking the Axis down.

While the media was tolerant of Eisenhower, they openly loathed Richard Nixon. Coming from California, he was twice vice-president under Dwight Eisenhower. He was an ardent anti-communist who earlier had investigated Alger Hiss. None of this earned him points with the eastern press establishment. They dubbed him "tricky Dick" and made his press interaction an uphill battle. On the contrary, in the presidential contest of 1960 Nixon was pitted against John Fitzgerald Kennedy from Massachusetts. JFK, the young, articulate and handsome Boston Brahmin, was the hands down favorite of the Eastern press intelligentsia. Even so, it was a very close vote in that election and one that Nixon could well have challenged *a la* Al Gore[24]. Instead he bowed out more gracefully than his later counterpart and would come back to successfully challenge Hubert Humphrey in the presidential contest of 1968.

There is no implication made here that all of this had any direct effect on me or on my life at that time. The political winds that swirled around the decade of the 1960's were only remotely and incompletely cognizant to a freshman entering high school. Nevertheless, there were ways in which I was affected by the greater sense of reality, or at least what I perceived to be reality, at the time.

I can faintly remember the televised presidential debates between Nixon and Kennedy. The sweaty forehead and the five o'clock shadowed face of Dick Nixon contrasted poorly with the cool and handsome face of the candidate from Massachusetts. Kennedy came off as a new, fresh answer to the problems of the day while Nixon seemed something out of the old, tired realm of the past. As a gullible adolescent viewer, I was impressed with the poise of this newer man and came away with a favorable opinion of him as a possible president. I would not know of the machinations of the television intermediaries until years later, and could not ascertain at the time, that the image had much to do with the positioning of those hot stage lights and the skill of the makeup men[25].

After the Kennedy victory, I was further impressed with the idealism of his inaugural address in January, 1961. That America "shall pay any price, bear any burden, meet any hardship, support any friend, oppose any foe to assure the survival and the success of liberty" resonated with me. It is noteworthy that the present day "liberals", who still consider JFK an icon, have apparently walked away from this commitment in the world. When he said, "Let the word go forth from this place, to friend and foe alike, that the torch has been passed to a new generation of Americans" it resonated with me and with many in my generation. His words were motivating for young people still struggling with their own identity. Like many, I was ready to comply when he said, "ask not what your country can do for you-ask what you can do for your country", even though I hadn't the faintest idea what it was that I should do at the time other than to finish high school.

The appeal to adolescent idealism is an appeal to a powerful urge. Unfortunately, the wisdom to sort out what form of action that idealism should take is sometimes trumped by the raw energy of the adolescent state. A common observation is that youth is wasted on the young. They do not know that maturity requires experience tempered by reason and that time is a necessity for its development. In particular, I did not know what direction my idealism should take but I was stirred by the exhortations of the new president and was eager to search.

There is little doubt that the example set by the new administration in our nation's capital was one reason that I got involved with school politics. As a former outsider, I ran for class president successfully in my freshman year and then for student council after that. In the junior and senior years I was elected president of the student council, where I became familiar with Robert's Rules of Order. Granted, there were no momentous issues in the high school at the time. We often joked with each other that most of our time was spent debating over decisions such as determining what soft drinks would be served at the school dances. During these years, this participation in student government also allowed me the opportunity to attend leadership training workshops, some of which were held at The University of Michigan. These experiences were extremely rewarding for me, since they reinforced the message that we attendees really were the "new generation" to whom "the torch" was passed. This idealistic approach appealed to my own sense of purpose and, as an added bonus, I met some very lovely members of the opposite sex at these conferences.

At Grosse Ile High School then, Marshall Gingrich was the principal and Bob Smith was the Superintendent of the district. I found the laconic Mr. Gingrich an interesting man to talk with and I tried to stay on his good side. This was a smart policy since he was legendary for being able to pin some of the toughest, misbehaving students up off the floor and against the lockers with one hand. Mr. Smith was a more talkative, outgoing man and I came to know and respect him by dating his daughter Jennifer for the last few years of high school.

Jennifer was my first love although not necessarily my first girlfriend. She was cute and popular and my Uncle Charley Randall, who never met her, looked at a picture of her once and said in his southern Indiana drawl, "she's a real dish, Steve". Jennifer was intelligent and had a common sense, warm approach to people and we did many enjoyable things together. There was a time when we even talked about being together long after high school, but that was not to happen. I have nothing but fond memories of her.

In retrospect, I feel that my secondary education prepared me well for my subsequent college studies. Once I realized the importance of the need to apply myself to the books, there was more than enough to challenge me during my high school years.

Overall, there was a general sense of seriousness communicated to the students by the teachers and administrators, so that everyone understood they were there to learn before all else. Sufficient amounts of home work were assigned, which helped me to learn to study and how to budget my time. Many students matriculate to college without good study habits and end up doing poorly as a result. That did not happen to me and I credit Grosse Ile High School for that. A high percentage of our high school graduates did attend college and I think most were well prepared for that step.

Several memorable teachers were the foundation for that preparation. To begin with, Mrs. Betty Sells, an excellent math teacher, had a very effective way of communicating a no-nonsense approach that intimidated even the most recalcitrant of us to pay attention and do well. My friend and team-mate Clyde Lowler was not easily intimidated, but he never crossed Mrs. Sells. I knew that her tough approach was something of a well-rehearsed act, since she was a very personable woman outside of the classroom. Nevertheless, the act was a good one and students learned math in her class.

Another fine instructor was Fred Robertson, who taught government and economics. He clearly enjoyed his students and knew how to get us involved in the discussions in his classroom. He used to explain that forms of government arrange themselves along a continuum. He then would write on the chalk board showing communism on the far left and fascism on the far right. That was fairly conventional logic, but as years of study and observation have gone by, I would now challenge that model. The continuum should be one of more freedom and less freedom, and on that scale both communism and fascism fall on one end.

The other notable teacher was Charles Strickler, my physics and chemistry teacher. He understood what he needed to teach and could explain scientific concepts well. However, apart from his subject matter, his stories of being transported over the pacific on the Queen Mary as a troop ship in WWII were a fascinating side light. According to his narrative, after about a week at sea, the soldiers found out that the rice that everyone had been eating had maggots in it. His description of all those men hanging over the sides and expelling their visceral contents was entertaining, to say the least.

Everyone has a favorite teacher that they may remember for anything from being a smart tutor of their subject matter, a good mentor of young people, or someone who was hard working and fair. Even downright good looks qualify in some cases. My most memorable teacher in high school was Fred Appleyard, who taught English and Literature. He loved what he taught and that was evident to his students. There was a sense of enthusiasm that he brought into the class each day. He loved to challenge us to think about what the great authors and poets meant by their writings and what deeper themes lurked behind the main lines. I can still envision him waving those dog-eared texts that were underlined twice and thrice in the air as he walked in front of the class trying to elicit a response to his questions. It is to him that I owe a great debt of gratitude, for I have a life-long love of some of those classics we read. To this day, I never tire of reading Shakespeare, Frost, Burns, Twain and others, and I thank him for it here.

Beginning in the junior high school years, Mom and Dad enrolled me in piano lessons at the Wyandotte conservatory. My instructor was Forrest Arnoldi, a wonderful piano player who performed professionally at one of the night clubs in Detroit. He wrote swing and jazz pieces for me which I played with increasing proficiency over time. Once, he took me to an outdoor performance of Duke Ellington's Band in Detroit. I remember shaking Duke's hand backstage after the performance. What a treat!

In high school, several of my friends also played musical instruments and we found ourselves putting together a band of our own, called "The Continentals". We actually performed at several of the weekend dances at the Youth Center on Meridian St. on the island. Our repertoire was about a half dozen rock and roll songs which included the Ray Charles hit "What I'd Say". Ray would not have cared for this rendition since, although we had the desire, we did not have the requisite talent to perform it well. Our contemporaries were lenient regarding our talent however, and we at least were not laughed off the stage. The Continentals included Dick Meyers on drums, Tom Lytle on tenor sax, Clyde Lowler on alto sax, Bob Bankovich vocals and me on piano. The fact that we all played football together made for a good transition as time went by. It was not long before we transitioned right out of music and right into sports on a permanent basis.

While there were other things that competed for attention, athletics was my real first love outside of school and family. Football to me was always first among the gods in the pantheon of sport, although basketball was a close second. I also went out for track, not because I had talent for the running events, but because it was good conditioning for the other two.

As a matter of fact, I remember track with particular anguish. Mr. Tissot, who was also the football coach, placed me in a number of events. In most meets I competed in the half mile, officially called the half-mile dash. True to its name, it was every bit a dash and not a run. Running at full speed for that distance always seemed like an unnatural act to me. Some runners are more natural at such things, but that was not the way I was made. The very first meet where I was entered in the half mile was unforgettable. It took place in Trenton, just across the river on the Trenton High School's cinder track. When the gun went off, the runners came out of the blocks so fast that I thought that I had mistakenly entered the 100 yard sprint rather than the half mile dash. I never ran the half mile during the four years of high school that I did not feel like stopping after the first time around the track. I never did stop and always finished the second lap since embarrassment was always something worse than physical discomfort.

Since football was the first god of sport to me, I increasingly approached it with almost ritual purity. I would train faithfully during the summers by running and throwing the football daily. Weight training was not generally used until my college years.

Nevertheless, I reported fit and ready for the preseason double sessions each year with progressive determination to do well at my position of quarterback on offense and halfback on defense. In those days at fairly small schools like ours, most players were prepared to go both ways.

In keeping with my personal athletic code, I also never smoked nor drank during high school. I had actually smoked considerably in my rebellious elementary school days. I used to steal away with a spare pack of my dad's cigarettes, find a tree in the woods, light up and puff away. Thankfully, the new found ardor of athletics changed that. I did not want to let myself or the team down by being less physically fit or mentally prepared than I could be. Smoking cigarettes and drinking alcohol were banned not so much by the authorities but by my own sense of dedication to the sport. I do not think I missed anything then and besides, there would come a time later on when I could experience some of those pleasures and vices.

I was fortunate to have many memorable moments during my high school athletic career. I do not do much reminiscing about specific plays or game situations. I tend to remember the whole process of the preparation and competition rather than scores of each and every contest. If pushed to recall any specific game situation, I might have to look back on the stat sheets to recall whether my memory serves me right. Just as there were outstanding teachers in the classroom, there were great coaches I remember. I give tribute here to Jay Tissot, the head football coach and Hal Goodhue, his assistant. Jay, in particular, had a quiet way about him that made you want to play to the best of your ability to gain his respect. Both of these fine men have my respect to this day.

Halfway through my sophomore football season, George Buelow, Dick Meyers and I were asked to go from junior varsity to varsity. I will never forget being sent into the game for my first play on the varsity squad. We were playing Flat Rock under the lights on their field and I was put in to receive a punt. Fortunately, I successfully fielded it and had a good runback of about 15 yards. It broke the ice for me and made me realize that I could compete at that level—perhaps at other levels as well. We won that game 33-26. In my junior year, I recall playing our nemesis from across the river in the town of Riverview. Their team had an all-state QB by the name of Lloyd Carr who threw the ball to a big tight end by the name of Jessie Jenkins. Carr and Jenkins went on to remarkable college careers and of course Lloyd Carr is now the head coach at The University of Michigan. We could not match up with that duo on that night and the final score was 27-13 in their favor.

George and I shared MVP awards our senior year, but I still had not had enough football. I decided I would play, even as a walk-on, after high school as well, even though our team records during my tenure on the Grosse Ile Red Devil football squad were not of championship caliber.

My years on the varsity basketball team were equally not remarkable from a win-loss standpoint. However, I was honored with the team MVP award for basketball my senior year. When I look back, it is with a great deal of satisfaction of having played and contributed during my high school career. The experience of being part of a team effort was something that has been valuable in later life. In the spring of 1964, I am proud to say that I won a post-season award given annually to an outstanding downriver high school athlete. It is known as the Willie Heston Award, named after a legendary halfback from The University of Michigan. I was honored to receive the award in an outdoor ceremony with my proud parents present. In the fall of that year I would matriculate at that same university.

Dad had been an elder in the Grosse Ile Presbyterian Church since its inception. Our family had regular church attendance but we had a tendency of being late for the services. Never shy, Dad would walk all the way up to the front rows, which were the only seats left on Sunday morning. The rest of us would sheepishly follow. Our family shares many funny stories having to do with Dad's ability to reach down the back ridge of the pews to quietly smack one of his giggling kids in the occiput. He was able to put an end to whatever foolishness was occurring without ever appearing flustered.

An important influence on me in those years was the new Presbyterian minister, Richard J. Milford. Mr. Milford came to the church soon after his divinity training. Urbane, well dressed, and a confirmed bachelor, he was a much different figure than what most expected from a minister. He was well educated with a Princeton Divinity Degree and a few years abroad for further training. His sermons were articulate and provocative and he was confident in his views. With regard to religion Dick was less fundamentalist in exegesis and emphasized the moral message of love manifested by the New Testament. Regarding current events his views were in keeping with those of the liberal left as far as civil rights, the great society poverty programs and later on the war in Southeast Asia.

Dick Milford and I became good friends, even though there was a separation of years in age between us. During my high school days I often accompanied him to concerts, dinners and even plays. On Saturdays, Dad traditionally made pancakes for the family and Dick was sometimes invited over for breakfast. When Dad and Dick had occasional discussions over social and political matters, they often disagreed vigorously and things could get testy.

Dick is included on the list of people whom I respect. I have learned many things from him over the years. He has always been a generous and caring friend to me. After marrying Kris, Dick became a welcome visitor to our home. We were always happy to see him during our time in Detroit. He has stayed current with our family life and likewise we have kept in touch with him over the years. We continue to look forward to his visits to our upper Michigan home when our schedules allow. We not only have the proud distinction of having him officiate at our wedding in 1969, but in 2004 he also presided at our daughter Erika's wedding in the same church.

It is time to connect the events of the greater world to my own. The process of high school advancement may be so sufficiently self absorbing that it could conceivably keep one solely focused on the particulars of the moment, so that the forest is not visible for the trees. In my case, it is expressly that self absorption that contributed to a world view which was inaccurate. The events that transpired in the country and in the world did not go unnoticed by me. I developed a definite approach to these events, in spite of the bustling pace of activity that engulfed me in the teenage years. All around me there was a reinforcement of the idea that my generation, our generation, was truly the "best and brightest" to come along. The president and his entourage were touted to be the smartest that the land could find and it seemed that all the really intelligent people in the country supported his approach to the problems of the day. To stray from that dogma was characterized as reactionary and antithetical to a "progressive" view of history. Many of us from the baby boom generation wanted to believe that this was true.

Well-meaning teachers and mentors had inadvertently given me an inflated impression about myself and about my generation which I may have misconstrued or only partially understood. Thus arose a perception that it was up to me and the members of my generation to find solutions to the problems we faced using reason (almighty reason) as our guide. The success that I had in school, in student government and in athletics seemed to support the same conclusion; namely that I was one of a generation of the truly best and brightest.

Implicit in this world view was the feeling that older generations may not have the answers that were needed. Therein, I now realize, exists a lack of humility and understanding about the obstacles our parent's generation (and others, of course) had already overcome. Unrecognized by us was the fact that it was precisely because our parents faced and vanquished those problems (i.e.-the depression, WWII), that their well-bred children could now have such feelings of self importance. Thus had arisen a *hubris* of mind which was going to have consequence for me later. As a tenet of the counterculture it would certainly have consequence for the nation.

# CHAPTER 4

## COLLEGE DAYS

The decision to attend the University of Michigan was mulled over for a long time but the choice was made certain by a remark made by my high school Spanish teacher, Miss Parks. That pretty first-year teacher asked me one day what colleges I was considering. In addition to Michigan, I had also entertained attending a few smaller schools where I was more likely to play football. Albion College, which had a very good academic reputation, was one of the places that I included as a possibility. When Miss Parks heard that she cleverly questioned, "So you're going to be a big fish in a little pond?" That inquiry rolled around in my head for a few days. I finally determined that I would indeed attend the U of M. I would be a little fish in a big pond! It was perhaps somewhat of a dare from that cute lady and I viewed it as such and took the challenge.

Dad had hoped that I might ultimately choose to attend school at Indiana University. We had taken several trips there to look it over. On one of those trips I attended a fraternity party with my cousin Dan Seitz, who was a student there. Dan eventually would go on to Indiana Law School and a successful career as a lawyer in that state. Indiana was not for me however. I left it to my brother Clyde, my sister Kim and my brother Raymond to be the Leonard legacy at that great university. In later years, Clyde graduated from IU in education, Kim in fine arts, and Raymond in business.

Without question, Ann Arbor was a "big pond". Traditionally, Michigan has attracted and admitted students from many parts of the country and the world. The University has prided itself on being a cosmopolitan school and has resisted the pressure to admit only students from the state of Michigan. It was the first time that I had met so many people from the coasts and from the Chicago area. Coupled with the intense academic competition to gain entry, the eclectic approach to education at Michigan created an arrogance of attitude in the student body. Michigan touted itself as "The Harvard of the Midwest", or as its students put it, "Harvard is the Michigan of the East". Probably because I had been on the campus before for visits and for high school student affairs, I was not particularly intimidated by the size of the university or by the conglomeration of student types that I saw.

Ann Arbor has always had a reputation for attracting many unconventional individuals. It was a real shock to see the most peculiar looking people wearing the most destitute looking clothing and then to find out that their family and personal wealth considerably dwarfed my own economic circumstances. The *faux* pauper chic of the sixties was not unnoticed by apparel manufacturers. They responded to that vogue back then and continue to do so now. Today one can purchase ready-made, shabby, ripped and faded attire at prices that would compete with those found on Rodeo Drive. The wardrobe of the "unconventional" is still sought after on many campuses.

I took up residence in the Allen-Rumsey House in the West Quadrangle, or "West Quad" as it was commonly known. On my first day I met my room-mates Bruce Getzan and Waino Pihl. We were all assigned together through a random selection process. Waino was a Michigan resident of Finnish extraction. He was enrolled in the school of Architecture and Design which was known to require considerable work outside of class. Bruce Getzan, who was from Denby High School in Detroit, was enrolled in the college of L.S.A. or Literature, Science and the Arts, as was I. His father was a union man so Bruce was a "dyed in the wool" Democrat. He idolized the Kennedy's and frequently played the album "Camelot" with Richard Burton and Robert Goulet on his record player. Waino had all he could do to keep up with the shenanigans that Bruce and I threw at him. We quickly learned the informal organization of the campus. We found that South Quad, across the street, was where the scholarship jocks lived, East quad was the home of the slide-rule-packing Engineers and "The Hill" was where the majority of the girls were housed. Those were the days before coed dormitories.

The decision to pursue a pre-medical course of study was a product of a long held impression that medicine would be a satisfying occupation. Ever since I was a little kid I thought that being a doctor might be a suitable combination of using one's intellect and also being able to interact with people. However, I had little practical knowledge about what medical doctors do since no one in my extended family was a doctor. I was not a science whiz kid who ran home every night to his chemistry set and I did not dissect frogs in my spare time. As a matter of fact, all the aptitude tests that I took in high school suggested that I was best fitted for language and verbal pursuits rather than math and science. Still, medicine seemed to be a career that a person could achieve through personal effort and which would allow individual initiative with regard to its practice. All along, I sensed that I did not want be part of a large organization like Ford Motor Company where I eventually realized that my Dad did not receive the recognition he should. Looking back on those days, I feel that my intuitions about these things were fairly correct.

To fulfill the medical school prerequisites and to leave time for other elective courses, I decided to major in Zoology. That would place me within the college of L.S.A. which had its own requirements as well, including two years of a foreign language. Attending my first day in the second year Spanish class, I was shocked when I introduced myself to the fellow sitting beside me. With a heavy accent, he replied that his name was Senor Piche and that he was from Madrid. It hardly seemed fair to be assigned Don Quixote, to be read and tested in Spanish, all the while competing with a native Spaniard. That, however, was the

U of M experience. One could either sink or swim. Fortunately, placing out of freshman English allowed me to take two semesters of Great Books, taught by Prof. Hopkins, a truly remarkable teacher. Because I thoroughly enjoyed these classes, I decided to minor in English.

However, the competition was fierce in my pre-med courses as students vied to maintain grades that would allow them to apply and be accepted to the various medical schools. Organic chemistry was then and presumably is now, a "cutter course". It was a necessity to do well in organic in order to get into medical school. In the lecture of over three hundred, students tried any technique to improve their standing and to set themselves apart from everyone else. The instructor for this class was Prof. Rasmussen, one of the smartest people I have ever known. From the moment that class began and until it ended, he wrote equations on the multiple black boards. With considerable alacrity, he proceeded through each session of class without a single misstatement and without a single note. Meanwhile, the students all scribbled desperately, trying to keep up with him in their personal notes. Many were unable to copy the equations from the board before he would begin to erase it to make room for new equations, a cause of some panic that he did not notice.

Prof. Rasmussen also quickly ended the perception that students could get a few extra points by arguing about their answers on his tests. After the first exam, when there was a long line outside his office during consultation hour, many students were eager to present their case that they were graded unfairly. Looking over the first few individuals' exams he would say that perhaps he could see where it might be reasonable to add an additional five points on the problem in question. Inevitably, he would then look at subsequent problems where he discovered that he had not subtracted sufficient points. He then made the numerical adjustment and handed the test paper back to the astounded student. A score that started out as a B+ usually devolved to a C+. All of a sudden the line at his office door dwindled to nothing.

The Undergraduate Library, known as the UGLI, was an unsatisfactory place to study. There were just too many distractions, not the least of which was the parade of coeds who marched by the study tables there and beguiled even the most dedicated of male students. The dorm was even worse since there was always some lonely "dormey" who wanted to squander the night and wanted company to do so. When I joined a fraternity, I found study conditions no better than the dorm, and possibly worse.

Although there are possibly some that can study in the midst of "creative confusion", I found that to be productive with my study time, I needed to find a really quiet place. The Graduate Library turned out to be an apropos location. Back in the stacks of the "Grad" were desks that were so cut off from reality that you literally could not tell whether it was day or night outside. The musty smell of old volumes of books was something to which the nose would quickly accommodate and the air seemed to hang like a veil of silence. I mentioned previously that Ann Arbor attracted "unconventional individuals". It seemed that an inordinate number of them spent time at the Grad and occasionally wandered by to disturb one's concentration. Spending extended hours in those stacks was definitely a Kafkaesque experience. Nevertheless, the Grad Library provided me with a calm, efficient place to learn and was my place of study for the duration in Ann Arbor.

Just as many of my collegiate academic experiences were memorable; my abbreviated experience with Michigan athletics was also unforgettable. Walking on to a division one squad was intimidating. The early team meetings left me with the impression that elite college football players are a physically unusual group. In overall size and stature, these guys were definitely more than two standard deviations from the mean, even in the days prior to widespread weight training. Coming from my small high school, I was not accustomed to seeing people of that physical stature, much less playing against them. The size, the strength, and the speed all combined to enforce my feelings of intimidation.

Gradually however, those feelings receded and I took my place down the pecking order and did my best to compete at my position. Back then, football was in my blood and I was determined to play out my aspirations.

A walk-on player like me was second fiddle to the recruited scholarship players. There was little likelihood that a non-scholarship player would make the first or second team, those likely to play in the Michigan Stadium on Saturdays. In the 1960's in the Big Ten, freshmen could not compete at the varsity level so freshmen teams practiced by themselves and had a few inter-squad scrimmages. Frequently, the freshmen competed with the varsity players, even though the varsity had enough bodies to have "hamburger" squads of their own. During the fall season there was pressure to prepare the first team defense and offense for the next opponent. The freshmen and the varsity subs were relegated to the role of giving the lead players real-time experience against the opposing system.

The freshman coach was Dennis Fitzgerald, a former Michigan player whose career was distinguished among other things, by the fact that he never played with a face mask on his helmet. This attribution to a code of toughness was accompanied by a tendency to scream every instruction he gave instead of talking in a normal voice. Most of the players tried to keep a space between themselves and Coach Fitz to avoid the inevitable blast of saliva that would accompany his commands.

In those days Chalmers "Bump" Elliot was the head coach of the Michigan varsity. His first assistant was Tony Mason. That combination amounted to the proverbial good cop-bad cop routine. As much of a gentleman as Coach Elliot was, and he was a genuinely good guy, Coach Mason was the antithesis. Coach Mason, as the prince of darkness, usually did not even acknowledge someone if they were a mere walk-on. He would, with some effort, try to minimize his surly demeanor for those who were on scholarship.

After winter conditioning and weight training, the team ramped up through the spring practices into game readiness. The culmination was the spring game which was played in the

Michigan stadium. It was exciting to get some playing time in that game and to complete a few passes to Larry Rogna, a tight end from Lansing. Larry was a captain of his state championship high school team. He and I became good friends and remain so today. We were fraternity brothers and room-mates for the rest of our college days. The fall of 1965 was to be my only season on a varsity football team. I never broke into the playing lineup on Saturdays that season, but dressed for all the home games. It was an unparalleled thrill to come into the "Big House" through the tunnel with the team and to hear the roar of 101,000 fans from ground zero. I will never forget the experience.

The fondest memories I have for college football at Michigan came on the Monday nights that followed the Saturday contest. In those days all the players who did not play on the preceding weekend would suit up for a full scale game. We called it "The Toilet Bowl" game. The squad was evenly divided into a "Blue" and a "Gold" team and the game took place across from the stadium at Ann Arbor High School under the lights. It was some of the best football I ever participated in and we went at it with great relish. The competition was keenly intense, since even in the backup ranks of Michigan football, the players were often of all-state caliber.

After completing the fall season of 1965, it became clear to me that it was unlikely that I would see serious playing time at Michigan. The demands of my studies and career plans certainly outweighed my commitment to football, so I decided to turn in my cleats. It was a passage of sorts for me, but one that from a career standpoint was logical and reasonable, both then and now.

My room-mate Bruce and I both decided to pledge a fraternity and we picked one right on State Street not far from our dorm. In those days Sigma Chi was known as one of the "jock" houses, since many members of the athletic teams were also members there. There turned out to be quite an assortment of other guys as well and it provided a dependable place for campus social events and camaraderie. Actually, the idea of having "brothers" seemed a bit trite since I already had real brothers at home.

However, I still consider many of my fraternity brothers good friends, with whom I have kept in touch. The memories of things that we did in Ann Arbor and trips that we took elsewhere resonate to this day. To try to list these fellows here would not do justice to them. A partial tally would include Larry Rogna, Bruce Getzan, Wayne Hanson, Elmo Morales, Al Krist, Bill Wood, John Kingscott and others.

In addition to college loans, I needed to find ways to help finance my education and living expenses. The demands of study would not allow full-time employment during the school year, but there were inventive part-time opportunities available. One of these jobs, prior to the era of enforced with-holding tax, social security deductions and employee benefits, was called a "meal job". A meal job was a widely utilized system around the campus that took many forms, but which basically entailed an exchange of work for food. For instance, I worked at a sorority house where I washed pots and pans for an hour or two and ate a meal that would be the main meal of my day. Kitchen work appealed to me more than having a waiter's job at the same place since the waiters were required to dress up in white shirt and tie to serve the more formally attired young women. Coming in after the meal was over, I washed the mountain of pots and pans, following which I ate a hearty feast. It seemed a fair trade on my time and effort. The cook was a friendly black woman and she always took care to save me some choice food in more than adequate quantity.

I also found some part time work in the medical records department of The University Hospital located on Observatory Drive. It accommodated the odd hours that I needed to work even though the pay was modest. Most of that work required moving charts from one place to another. It did not require any real medical training, which as yet I did not have anyway. However, this job revealed to me another particularly easy way to earn money. The blood bank at the hospital paid $20 for a donation of one unit of blood. Of course, in that day there was no concern over the transmission of Hepatitis B and C and it preceded the discovery of HIV. Thus, neither the units nor the donors required extensive screening. It was always a good feeling to walk out of that blood bank with a crisp twenty dollar bill in my pocket. In those days that amount could really buy something and I availed myself of the opportunity to give blood as often as I could, within the guidelines of the blood bank.

My summer jobs supplied the real help that I needed to finance my education during the four years of undergraduate training. In the summer between high school and college, Dad found Curt Crysler, my best friend from high school, and me a job at the 1964 World's Fair located in Flushing, New York. He also found an apartment for us that could be sub-let in lower Manhattan. The Lower East Side of Manhattan was a world apart from what we knew as small town suburban kids. We quickly became familiar with the subway system and every day at 2PM we boarded the 14th St.-Canarsie Line to begin our trip under the East River, up through Queens and finally to the Fairgrounds in Flushing. We worked the afternoon shift at a glorified hot dog stand at the fair and the work was not particularly hard. There we became acquainted with some of our co-workers who happened to live in Harlem, one of whom was named Juanita. On one occasion she invited us to a party after work at her apartment, so we accompanied her home. Needless to say, we were the only white faces on the trains that night and although we were apprehensive about our safety, nothing untoward happened.

Coming back from work to our rental apartment on 12th St. on the Lower East Side was an interesting experience almost every night. Our neighborhood was heavily Puerto Rican and the bars were always hopping by that time, usually about 2AM. Frequently, while we were walking from the subway station toward our apartment, a bar door would crash open and the bartender or bouncer would literally throw an unruly patron out into the gutter of the street, right in front of us. It was like being transported back to the Wild West, only this was Manhattan in the 1960's. All said, Curt and I had a marvelous time in NYC. At that time in our young lives it was hard to catalog what we may have learned from the experience. We shared mutual and great expectation as the summer wound down, since we were both enrolled at the University of Michigan for the fall. There Curt earned an engineering degree and now works in international sales. He still lives on Grosse Ile with his wife Nancy, whom he met at Michigan.

One of the hardest jobs I ever had was in the summer of 1966. My brother Clyde, who was headed to college at IU in the fall, and I were hired at a clay drain tile manufacturing company near Flat Rock Michigan. I then owned a Honda 160 motorcycle for transportation, which we rode there together every morning for the start of work at 7 AM. It was a small company and there were not more than a dozen employees. Our job involved the transfer of drain tiles from the kiln pallets to the wooden pallets for transport. We picked up four tiles in each hand and lifted them over to the pallets with each transfer. We did that for eight hours each day, allowing fifteen minutes for each of the morning and afternoon breaks and thirty minutes for lunch. We were not paid any thing near what the UAW union wages were at Ford, yet it seemed we worked ten times as hard. Clyde and I knew we had put in a full day's labor when we made our way home each afternoon. Those were the kinds of jobs that reinforced the incentive to stay on course in our college studies.

Dad was able to get me on at Ford Motor Company for several jobs including a summer at the Rouge Frame Plant where I worked in the quality control department as a welding inspector on the frame line. This was a real eye opener, since I was exposed to the mentality of "don't make waves and don't bust your butt, because it might make someone else look bad". When there was a break in the action, my foreman told me to "get lost" behind a machine and read a book. He made it very clear that I should not be seen by the supervisors that walked through the plant because it would cause problems for him if I was seen not actively working.

When I was told to sweep the floor, I swept it like I normally would. Ray Leonard certainly had taught his sons how to sweep the floor and to do it well. This drew comments from other co-workers to "slow down" and "don't kill the job".

There were some hard physical jobs at the frame plant and I recall seeing in particular a well-built black man who transferred front end assemblies from the machine welder to the production line. He lifted those heavy frames steadily through his shift and there was no question that he worked for his pay.

Many jobs however, seemed to allow an excess of "slack" and "screw off" time. Absenteeism was a problem in the plant, particularly on the day after payday. On Fridays, prior to the weekend break, the inspectors had to watch carefully that beer cans were not welded into the frames. Shoddy work was a problem on the frame line and substance abuse contributed to it. One welder was constantly reaching for his thermos which contained vodka mixed with juice. One day I was relieved from my job to be transported over to the union hall. There was a union election and there was no question for which candidate I was expected to cast my vote, since I was instructed carefully by the plant union rep as he drove me there.

My experience at the frame plant was a real slice of reality. I could not help but think about it later in the 1970's and the 1980's when the auto companies worried about the Japanese competition, and again in 1979 when Chrysler executives asked for and received a federal subsidy or bailout of their company. It seemed to me that the problems of the auto plants needed other solutions than just a taxpayer underwrite[26].

In 1967, John Kingscott, Bill Wood and I decided to take a road trip to Alaska later in the summer and in order to put together a "grubstake" for the trip we needed to work for six or eight weeks. Kingscott and I found work at the GM Hydramatic plant. At the time, "Johnny Ringo", as he was called, owned an old Triumph motorcycle and I owned an old rusted ragtop Oldsmobile. We alternated our respective modes of transportation to Willow Run for the afternoon shift each day. Traveling tandem down I-94 on a motorcycle at night was one thing, but backing up that big red ragtop was another. The Oldsmobile's reverse gear did not engage well. Not having reverse gear became a problem when I pulled the car into a parking spot in the lot for each night's shift. Getting out of the slot after the shift was over required John to keep his foot on the brake pedal while the engine was running while I crawled under the car. With a channel lock pliers I manually turned the drive shaft leading to the transmission over into reverse. Once done, we would back up and head out of the lot as if we were in a normal car; only, we knew that this was not a normal car.

The trip to Alaska that summer was one that I will remember for a lifetime. Bill Wood had a Volkswagen beetle that logged 11,000 miles on that jaunt with us "three amigos" inside. We had sleeping bags and slept out under the stars each night since we could not afford other accommodations. We lived off fresh bread from the bakeries in the small towns we crossed and cheap port wine from the local stores. We headed up across Canada to Dawson Creek, British Columbia, the start of the Alkan Highway. At that time the road was still gravel, 1400 miles of it in fact. The semi's that rolled up and down the highway threw rocks every which way, so we had to put plastic covers over the head lights to keep them from breaking. Even with that, the wind shield ended up with eleven cracks from the trip.

Alaska was bigger and wilder than anything that we had seen in the continental states. The roads went only half way up the state and it took plane or boat to see much of the remainder of its territory. These were both modes of travel that we could not afford. The grandeur of Mt. McKinley and of the Glaciers around Anchorage was breathtaking and we marveled at all of this, as young men would. From the radio we learned that in Detroit a riot broke out on 12th Street and spread so fast that the National Guard was called in to stop the looting and restore order. That news was a marked contrast from what we were seeing up there, and it was a cold splash of water across our collective face[27] .

The interaction that I had with my family after enrolling at Michigan was fairly infrequent, especially if one considers the short distance from Ann Arbor to my home on Grosse Ile. My work load during the school year and the demands of football early on left the summers as the only sustained visits with my parents and siblings. The times that Clyde and Mark snuck away from home to visit with me in Ann Arbor often exceeded my own visits home. Clyde, and his high school girlfriend and future wife Sue, often found a way to cut out of school on Friday's and make the trip by motorcycle to Ann Arbor. It was always a cheerful surprise to see them waiting when I returned to my room from classes.

Mark also visited me in Ann Arbor later on in those years. Often when he did, he was wearing a shirt that he had filched from my suitcase during my last trip home. He was not deterred one bit by the fact that I recognized my clothing and he could invent exculpatory explanations for how he came by it, almost on the spot. In our family, there was general agreement that Mark was the recipient of the thespian genes handed down from Ralph Leonard to his son Ray. However, it seemed to us that the genes were considerably embellished before they were then dispatched to grandson Mark.

A significant milestone in my Dad's career was a run for the 15th Congressional seat in the election of 1964. Some Michigan Republicans he knew approached him and asked him to enter the race against John Dingell in that downriver district. Dingell was the son of the previous congressman from the same district and shared the exact same name, something tantamount to a double incumbent's advantage. Once Dad decided to run, he delved into the race in characteristic Ray Leonard fashion. He went to plant gates and businesses where he shook hands and handed out campaign literature. He was a man from management who did not shrink from asking for the hourly man's vote in what was a heavily Democrat district.

On the state level, the governor's race included George Romney on the republican ticket, who went on to win with 55% of the vote. The presidential race was between Lyndon Johnson, the Democrat, and a Republican senator from Arizona known as Barry Goldwater. The Democrats portrayed Goldwater as a war monger because of his support for bombing the North in the war in Vietnam. This strategy worked and in Michigan, Johnson's coattails helped the old style liberal Dingell in the election[28]. If the year was 1966, those coattails might have been less effective. In that mid-term election, with a less popular LBJ as president, the Democrats lost 47 seats in the house. Ray Leonard made a good showing in the November '64 voting and even made some inroads in the union households. However, it was not enough to overcome the odds and the election went to Dingell. Dad returned to his job and life continued on in the Leonard home as before. It is of interest that John Dingell is now the longest running member of the House of Representatives, having won 24 elections straight.

In the fall of my senior year at Michigan, I made application to medical school. I applied and interviewed at both Michigan and at Wayne State. During the nervous interval between application and response, I submerged myself in my senior year academic pursuits. After the inevitable waiting process, I was notified of my acceptance at Wayne State and of my placement on the waiting list at Michigan. Those were the days before affirmative action and other preferential admission practices, so I have to assume that I did not make the grade at my alma mater. Wayne State had a good reputation for teaching clinical medicine and since I did not anticipate a research career in medicine it may have actually been the better of the two choices. It was exciting to look forward to the next stage of my training, and it seemed that everything was in place for me to reach the goals that I had set so many years previously.

It is of interest to me, looking back on the decade of the 1960's, to assess how my own view of the greater world was evolving from my adolescent high school years to my young adulthood years as I finished college. The news of the death of JFK on November 22, 1963, occurred when I was in English class during my senior year of high school. Like many others of my generation it had a profound effect on me. Abraham Lincoln once wrote a letter of condolence to Fanny McCullough, the daughter of his long-time friend William McCullough, on the occasion of her father's death in the Civil War. He said in part that "In this sad world of ours, sorrow comes to all; and to the young, it comes with bitterest agony, because it takes them unawares. The older have learned to ever expect it."[29] Lincoln's words resonate with regard to the impact of the assassination of John F. Kennedy on the baby boom generation. That event left an indelible mark on the young "to whom the torch [had been] passed" and may in some ways have skewed many in their subsequent views of the national and world situation. His death certainly had that effect on me. It is ironic that a statement of the 16th president who also met death at the hands of an assassin is so germane to the death of the 35th president similarly taken.

JFK's assassination, occurring in my high school days, shaded my subsequent exposure to the political milieu of Ann Arbor in my college years. Some students at The University of Michigan considered themselves in the vanguard when it came to campus controversies and at that time there were many tempests to weather. Tom Hayden, the former editor of The Michigan Daily in 1960, was a local student activist who also became the head of Students for a Democratic Society (SDS) by1962[30]. In December, 1967, Mario Savio spoke on the steps of The Michigan Union, and to a crowd of 2000 on the Diag[31]. He was the nominal leader of the Berkeley Free Speech Movement that began in 1964, which had confronted their administration with a mass sit-in and protest. Extracting concessions from Clark Kerr, then the president of Berkeley, activists were interested in spreading the "free speech" movement to other campuses. The number of students that actually belonged to these campus political groups was quite small, but many other students were aware of them and were at least somewhat sympathetic to their aims. What aims they had were not always clear, since at their core the activist groups shared a general disdain of traditional American values and sought to link issues like the Vietnam war with student free speech rights, as well as civil rights.

In 1965 the first anti-war demonstration occurred at the University of Michigan and was followed by a national anti-war march in Washington, D.C. the same year[32]. During this period there were also "teach-ins" on campus which portrayed the war effort in a decidedly anti-US fashion. Although I did not attend these demonstrations, I was starting to accept the portrayal of the war as a misguided affair that really amounted to a civil war among the North and South Vietnamese, and as such, we should not interfere. This was the standard analysis that was shared by the left then and even now.

Portraying the war as an erroneous use of American power was abetted in this era by our own elected representatives. Congressional Democrats began to distance themselves from this intervention which was started and escalated by their own party during the administrations of Kennedy and Johnson. In 1965, the "Doves", led by Senate Foreign Relations Chairman Fulbright, began to call for a temporary halt to air strikes against the North. Shortly thereafter Senator Frank Church called for direct negotiations with the North Vietnamese. In 1966 Fulbright's committee held extensive hearings, known as the "Vietnam Hearings", which were televised to the public. While witnesses for the administration, in particular Secretary of State Dean Rusk, made a poor case for the American role in Southeast Asia, academic types like Professor Henry Steele Commager complained that current American Policy had caused a "sense of disillusionment and alienation in the intellectual community".

The congressional "Hawks", typified by Senator and failed presidential candidate Goldwater, included most Republicans and some (mostly Southern) Democrats. They criticized Johnson's war effort of "gradualism", which allowed the North Vietnamese to recoup from every loss, and called for bombing of the North and its sanctuaries. Generally, they supported unleashing our Naval and Air power but balked at the enlargement of our own ground forces. However, under Senate Minority Leader Everett Dirksen's direction they stopped short of wholesale criticism and continued to support the Johnson policies. This conundrum made ineffectual any real change in the prosecution of the war.

The result of these deliberations meant that the direction of the U. S. war aims defaulted from seeking victory to maintaining the status quo of gradualism. During this period the majority of public opinion actually supported the war, but with an ineffective strategic plan to continue its prosecution, that support slipped[33]. Moreover, the tenor of the congressional debate inexorably chipped away at the previous broad consensus of both political parties for the active use of American power in the Cold War. The hesitation to project American strength and the "blame America first" attitude is increasingly characteristic of the modern day liberal Democrats. This divide in the political culture has persisted to the present day and even after the end of the Cold War. In the 1960's our congressional leaders fecklessly acquiesced to the criticisms that emanated from the anti-US political left, which included the campus left. This linking of a failing war effort to a fundamental shift in thinking about America's role in the world was just what the student activists wanted. They were eager to make even further links to their overall criticism of American society.

By the time Richard Nixon came into the executive office in 1968, the veiled criticism of the war from the "Doves" in congress and in the public became a torrent of protest. He was given little time or support to deal with the extrication of the U.S. from its commitment in Vietnam. Thus, he inherited the fool's errand of instituting the policy of "Vietnamization". This unrealistic policy entailed helping the South Vietnamese take over their countryside and its governance in the face of an undeterred invasion from the North.

The press, who always despised Nixon, caviled louder and added to his difficulty. The reporting of Walter Cronkite relating to the successful Tet offensive in 1968, where U.S. Marines overwhelmingly repulsed the North Vietnamese invasion, is well known. Cronkite reported the news of that unmitigated victory as if it were an abject defeat and added to the cacophony of critics calling for withdrawal[34]. As a result of these influences, the House of Representatives passed a resolution in December, 1969 which called for "peace with justice", and the course seemed clear what that would portend.

The denouement of my undergraduate years at Michigan was marked by several additional critical events. Martin Luther King,

Jr. was assassinated early in 1968, triggering national demonstrations, including a peaceful vigil near the Diag of the UM campus. I attended this and spoke with Derrick Humphries, a young black student who was also a former teammate of mine. I found little to say to him about this sad occurrence, and found myself sheepish talking about it. This was my first personal experience with collective white guilt. I not only felt sad about the needless death, I also felt ashamed about it, as though all whites had killed him and I should take some of the blame. It is not that Derrick intended me to feel that way, because I do not think he did. I respected Derrick as a player and as a person. Perhaps other black students at the vigil did feel that way about the whites in attendance, perhaps not. There, I learned personally how formidable was truthful talk between the races. It is still awkward for blacks and whites to discuss events that bear on the subject of race. It is difficult to be candid with each other and devoid of guilt or anger.

In the presidential race of 1968 the Democrat primaries were a real battleground. Johnson was shocked when Eugene McCarthy, a senator from Minnesota, won 42% of the vote in the New Hampshire primary in comparison to his 49%. When it looked like McCarthy would beat him in Wisconsin, LBJ pulled out and announced his decision not to run for re-election. McCarthy also beat Robert Kennedy in the Oregon primary in May, but in June Bobby Kennedy was assassinated. McCarthy was an outspoken opponent of Johnson and the war. He called the Vietnam War "unmorally unjustified". As a political and social maverick, he had considerable appeal to students at that time. He eventually lost the nomination to Hubert H. Humphrey at the turbulent Democrat convention in Chicago that summer. Many protestors clashed with police outside the convention hall and the level of violence there was disconcerting to the country, serving to escalate the tensions between supporters and protestors of the war across the land.

Many college students supporting McCarthy were going "clean for Gene" by shaving their beards and mustaches and cutting their hair to a suitable length. I joined a group that supported him from U.M. and we went door to door in northern Indiana campaigning for Gene[35]. Much to the chagrin of my parents, I missed my own graduation ceremony in order to do so. Armed with the moral certitude that I had acquired in Ann Arbor over the previous few years, I was confident that missing my graduation was a small price to pay for such a noble effort in support of this valiant candidate from Minnesota. After all, it seemed that so many students, faculty and residents of Ann Arbor agreed with the exegesis of the war according to Saint McCarthy. Such were the conclusions of that day. Many years later, my own son Zachary would attend The University of Michigan as an undergraduate. Not long ago, he told me that his friends had a definition for Ann Arbor which was "10 square miles surrounded by reality". How much has been learned in just a generation!

Immediately after graduation, my student deferment changed and I was reclassified as 1-A for the military draft. Dutifully, I went for my physical to Fort Wayne in Detroit and passed the exam easily. When I enrolled in medical school at Wayne in the fall, my draft board received that notification and I was reclassified 2-S.

In the meantime, I set about to earn money for living expenses by working two jobs. The afternoon shift job was at the Ypsilanti Ford Plant as a guard at the front gate. The work was fairly easy, the hourly pay from Ford Motor Company was better than most other summer jobs that I could find and Ford supplied me with the official looking guard's uniforms. Earlier during the day, I worked a part time job at Follett's Bookstore, which was the main student bookstore in Ann Arbor. I loaded books off the trucks at the rear loading docks and on snack breaks I became acquainted with a pretty cashier in the front of the store. Working that second job led to the most fortunate thing that happened to me in my four years at U.M., and in my life. I fell madly in love with that pretty girl, whose name was Kristine Ellen Erickson. Within the year, she would become my wife. That is a story yet to be told.

# CHAPTER 5

## MEDICAL SCHOOL
## AND MARRIAGE

M eeting Kris brought a fortuitous and happy close to my last summer in Ann Arbor. Our first official date was a daytime picnic trip to a local lake for sun and swimming. It is no exaggeration to say that we were attracted to each other from the start. While at the lake, she told me a little white lie about having to get home early that evening to meet her mother, who was coming for a visit. Actually, she had a prior date with a guy she had been seeing and her mother was not expected until the next day. By the end of the afternoon, she felt she should tell me the truth about her date. When she did, I told her that I understood and that I would be sure to get her home in plenty of time. From that time forward, we dated each other exclusively.

The remainder of the summer and the early fall was an enchanting time for us. We spent every extra moment together; talking, walking, dining and getting to know what dreams we each had for our future. Kris was entering her senior year at Michigan and would graduate in the following spring. We were excited with the possibilities of what a life together might bring and we were falling deeper in love by the day. In less than seven weeks from our first meeting we decided that we would marry that next year. It is with amazement that we both look back at that whirlwind romance and how it has resulted in thirty-five interesting and happy years of marriage. In later years, we did not readily disclose the details of this romance to our own children, fearing that they might emulate us. The odds of such a precipitous decision being successful still seem slim, even to us.

Just prior to the start of medical school, I needed to find lodging in Detroit and chose to locate downtown, not too far from Wayne's medical school. At that time the school was just across the I-75 Freeway from the old Detroit General Hospital. That in turn was adjacent to the Detroit Police Department and the City Jail. Greek Town was a few blocks away. The character of inner city Detroit was just about as far removed from the aura of Ann Arbor as the moon is from the earth. I found an attic apartment on Prentiss St. just off the main campus of Wayne State and just north of the Cass Corridor. The Cass Corridor was an urban slum at that time and those who lived there were universally poor and on bad times. Furthermore, in terms of crime rates, it is an understatement to say that I could have found safer places. However, the impervious nature of youthful thought left that consideration out of the equation. Prentiss St. was to be my first year's home in "Motown".

As it continues to be now, medical school was roughly divided into two years of pre-clinical work and two years of clinical experience. Much of the first two years was a continuation of undergraduate schooling and was heavily academic and book related. Those years were filled with basic science and human physiology and proceeded to a study of various disease processes and their nomenclature. In the first year we took gross anatomy and dissected our own cadavers in small groups. The inevitable testing process was so frequent and unnerving that most medical students could have made a career of designing impossible tests for a professional testing service if their medical studies were to ever go awry. Although there was a smattering of clinical medicine in those early years and although physical diagnosis was taught then, most of what people imagine medical school to be took place in the second two years. That is, the last two years were concerned with assigned and elective rotations through the hospitals and clinics. This is where the student experiences the various specialties, such as medicine, surgery, pediatrics, obstetrics, and others.

Wayne State Medical School is perhaps less well known than many other schools around the nation. It has the reputation among its students of being strong in its clinical material and less research oriented than others. This characterization is likely unfair since there are many outstanding research-oriented individuals on its considerable faculty. From the student's perspective however, it carries the "Avis rental car-we try harder" reputation. Most students are happy knowing that they will likely be competitive in matching with their residency choices and that Wayne will give them a solid background in assessing and dealing with sick patients.

Wayne's Medical School was established earlier than is generally known. It was founded in 1868 and has grown over a century and a half to over 1000 students, 800 full time faculty and 2000 part time clinical faculty members[36]. It is now affiliated with the Detroit Medical Center and through coordination of its teaching experiences with a total of fourteen hospitals in the greater metropolitan area. Thus, its students have a wealth of patients and hospital settings and this certainly contributes to why its students have the reputation for being clinically well grounded. About half of its graduates enter residencies in the primary care specialties. Many physicians from Wayne State end up practicing in Michigan. In Southeastern Michigan alone, 60% of the physicians in practice have trained partially or fully at Wayne[37].

My own class at Wayne State numbered 126 upon Graduation in 1972 and just somewhat more at the start in 1968. The emphasis in medical school was not, and still is not, on whittling down the number of matriculating students to a smaller number by graduation. The old pyramid system of "look beside you— that person probably will not be here four years from now", no longer pertains. It was assumed that those offered a spot in the entering class could do the work and had the intelligence to finish. Currently, one of every eleven medical school applicants nation wide applies to Wayne State and the pool of applicants have always contained many who were not successful gaining entry but who could have academically completed the required work.

Students tended to gravitate to small groups for social interaction and camaraderie because of the large class size and the spread out urban nature of Detroit. It was not that one did not interact with everyone in the class since we all knew each other on a first name basis. It was rather that the interaction was only superficial with many class mates due to the distances between the various living arrangements that were made and the interests that were shared. Regardless of that, my attention outside of the classroom for the first year was intensely focused on a pretty blond, my fiancé, who was in Ann Arbor.

Prior to starting medical school, I traded in my motor cycle for a (very) used Austin-Healy Sprite. The best that could be said about it was that it ran, and unlike another car I had owned, actually had a reverse gear. It was noticeably rusted out, particularly around the driver seat and passenger seat floor boards. This was coupled with the fact that the convertible top was torn and was repeatedly repaired with the poor student's old friend, "duct tape". It was not that I was partial to rust and torn rag tops, but rather that given my financial situation, those were the types of cars that met the contingencies of my budget. The condition of that car made driving or riding in it a very close to nature experience. The wind would whistle in through the floor and the top and kept the inside temperature close to ambient. Kris and I packed old wool blankets along the floor, but on our frequent trips on I-94 between Ann Arbor and Detroit, this made little difference. Those jaunts through the fall and winter of that first year recall particularly cold memories for both of us. It would be corny but true, to paraphrase the words of the song, "we had our love to keep us warm".

Our engagement flew by and I did well during that year of med school and Kris did equally well in her final undergraduate year. Earlier in the fall I met her mother Muriel and her Aunt

Claire in Ann Arbor. Since I was from the Lower Peninsula of Michigan and had traveled to the Upper Peninsula only several times previously, I had only a few acquaintances from there. It was an amazement to find how many of Kris' friends were in the Ann Arbor-Detroit area. On various occasions when I walked around Ann Arbor with Kris, she inevitably greeted or pointed out students who were from the UP. By contrast, I would hardly ever run into people from downriver Detroit in similar circumstances. My visit to her home in Iron Mountain at Christmas gave me a chance to meet her family and friends and get to know more of what made my future bride who she was.

Kris' father, E.O. "Buck" Erickson, was the former sports editor and general editor of the local paper, "The Iron Mountain News". For decades he was an avid promoter of the local ski jumping classic which annually drew competitors from all over the world. His extensive and lively coverage of that event over the years resulted in his induction into the Ski Hall of Fame, which is now located in the Upper Peninsula town of Ishpeming. He was proud of his daughter, whom he called "tine" (pronounced teen). When he told me to "make sure to keep her smiling", I assured him that to the best of my ability, I would.

Kris' mother Muriel was the kind of woman who would immediately make someone feel right at home after meeting them. She was known and respected by almost everyone whom I ever met that knew her. She was a woman of many talents and, although she had not attended college, she was very intelligent. It was abundantly clear that Kris had inherited many good things from this fine woman. Having previously worked at the VA Hospital in Iron Mountain, Muriel worked at that time at the local county hospital, so she was pleased that I was going into a medical career. Later, she became my first receptionist and all around organizer in setting up my medical practice. She actually interviewed and hired my first office nurse Sherry (Marquette) Johnson who, as a dear friend and employee, is still with my practice today. Muriel's connections in the medical community of that area were invaluable.

Kris' only sibling was a brother, whose name was Charles D. "Chuck" Erickson, and who was married to a school teacher named Karen. Chuck had a life long love of heavy machinery and was working at the Bacco Road Construction Company when I met him. He was also a member of the National Guard between the years 1963-1970. During that time, in the summer of 1967, he was with the Guard units that were deployed to Detroit. After getting shot at, while trying to put fires out, he had little love for the city where I was attending school. He made those feelings quite clear and was outspoken about many other things such as dress, facial hair, lifestyle, etc. Chuck had had many colorful experiences thus far in his young life. His path had differed considerably from mine. Because we did not have many things in common, Chuck and I were initially like oil and water. That would change considerably over time. Now, having known him over thirty-five years, I consider him to be a true friend and a brother.

Kris' family on her mother's side resided in Norway, Michigan, just six miles from Iron Mountain. Both sides of her family were 100% Swedish. Her Grandfather Charles Johnson came to the United States at the age of twelve. He was a well respected, hard-working carpenter. Before he was married he worked in the woods as a logger. He would literally walk to the logging camp in Hardwood from his home in Norway on Sunday evening, live in the camp during the week with the crew and walk back to his home in Norway after work on Saturday, a distance of 30 miles each way. His subsequent construction jobs required similar treks, which he made without complaint. I never met Kris' grandfather since he had already passed away by the time that I met her, but everyone in the family had loving memories of that stalwart man. Kris considered him one of the "rocks" in her life and missed him dearly.

Her Grandmother Ellen survived her husband for many years, living in her home in Norway with her daughter Claire and frequently with her son Carl. Their daughter Selma Putnam moved back home to live after her second husband Grady died, staying there until her own death at 87. Carl died soon after Selma. Claire, who after her retirement from teaching, was a caretaker for her siblings for many years. She still lives at the same residence. The fact that a son and two daughters of Charley and Ellen lived their later years in the home in which they were born, says something about the stability and deep roots of this remarkable family.

Kris' grandfather owned a 40 acre farm in the outer parts of the town of Norway. That land, named "the camp", included farm fields and woods. The wooded areas varied from lowland creeks and swamps to upland rocky hills and hardwood stands. It was a family treasure that was passed on to Kris' brother Chuck, who then also purchased two additional 40's adjacent to the original farm. This land became home for Chuck and he happily continues to maintain and care for "the camp" to this day. During my first visit at Christmas time in 1968, I only began to understand the various strands of Kris' family life. What I saw made me ever more interested in the girl I would soon marry.

Just six months later, on June 21, 1969, Kris and I were married in Iron Mountain. The service took place at Our Savior's Lutheran Church where she and her family were members of the congregation. Kris had already met my friend Dick Milford and we both wanted him to officiate at the ceremony, which was followed by a reception at the Pine Mountain Resort.

I approached this date with a somewhat cavalier attitude, thinking it would be no problem going through such a ceremony. In my naiveté, I had not considered the momentous nature of marriage and the serious side of taking vows for life. Thus, I was woefully unprepared for how the process of getting married would really play out for me.

I should have known that things would be difficult when I went for my last haircut as a single guy. This occurred in Wyandotte Michigan just prior to driving North for the wedding. I was home with my family at the time and my Dad offered to take me to his favorite barber in an adjacent town. Dad loved to chat with people and was a natural at meeting someone and within just a short period of time he would know just about everything about them and their families. On this occasion, no sooner had we gotten in the door of the barbershop than Dad started the conversation. The barber who was no small talker himself responded and turned the barber's chair away from the mirror so I could not see the work in progress. They talked on and on and he cut while he spoke. When the haircut was over the barber took the drape off and proudly turned me to the mirror to show me his handy work.

I was so shocked by my appearance that I was speechless. The cut was short, which was expected, but the left side was higher than the right and there were uneven areas all over. The barber wished me good luck with the wedding and I nodded my assent as we left. We drove home while I wondered how I could show up for my own wedding looking like that. As it turned out, worry about my hair was an over reaction and my appearance was not an impediment to anything significant, merely a sign of my general nervousness about the upcoming ceremony.

The pre-wedding haircut has another sidelight of interest. Thereafter, Kris became my resident barber. Cutting hair turned out to be another of her many talents and she has cut my hair ever since. I have not gone back into a barbershop or salon, as they may now be called, even though I am certain that that particular barber has probably retired or passed away.

Our wedding day was sunny and clear. The church was beautifully prepared and both Dick Milford and Pastor Grandquist participated in the service. Kris was, as expected, a lovely bride who, according to tradition, was kept closeted from my view that day until she was escorted down the aisle. Reciting our vows together, she seemed more constrained than I, as my voice cracked in my responses. At the end of the wedding I remember the tears as I hugged my Dad in the back of the church, tears I had not expected. I was surprised by my own emotion at that moment, not realizing it was in part a culmination of my youthful lack of mental preparation for the event. The reception was a welcome respite for me and a time to regain my equilibrium as we celebrated with our family and friends.

We could not afford much of a honeymoon, so our options were limited. Pastor Grandquist generously offered the use his cottage, which was near Duluth, Minnesota. The weather was cold and rainy, as it often is in the spring in the upper Midwest. There was not much to do from a recreational standpoint, but we made the best of it. There were only several days before we needed to get back to Lower Michigan. Although our wedding ceremony was flawlessly executed and the date is the most significant of my life, the event of our wedding and honeymoon was not as pleasantly memorable for me as was my prior courtship of Kristine and our subsequent marriage.

Just one week after our wedding, my brother Clyde and his high school girlfriend Susan Cook were married. Two weddings in the Leonard family in as many weeks provided a great deal of travel and activity for everyone.

Prior to our marriage, Kris found a teaching job in one of the high schools in the suburb of St. Clair Shores. Before meeting me, she had intended to work in journalism, possibly abroad. However, when our plans for a future together crystallized, she determined that a career in teaching would be a more practical plan of employment to help her husband through the financial drain of medical school. For our first year together we lived in St Clair Shores, but then moved back downtown to an apartment on Fourth Street, from which she commuted to work each day. Several times when the harried, busy English teacher left for school, she glanced at her husband, the perennial student, propped up studying in a chair and flashed one of those looks that said, "You really owe me!" She was right and I did.

Fourth Street was one of those unusual streets that resulted from the interruption of a city street by freeways. It was a one block stretch located adjacent to the intersection of the Henry Ford and the John Lodge freeways, with a motley combination of brownstone flats, apartment buildings, a church and a few private homes. This section was located just north of the Main Campus of Wayne State and, like most of the housing in that area, it was pretty run down. We lived in a second floor flat of a brownstone with a porch in the front. Often when we sat on that porch, closed our eyes, and listened to the constant roar of cars on those freeways, we pretended that the rumbling of the passing cars was the sound of ocean waves. Confined to the atmosphere of the city, we used imagination to temporarily transport us away. Besides, even then it was hard to find ocean front property at such good rental rates.

To our naive minds, we considered the street to be reasonably safe. We lived there for four years, creating many good memories of our escapades during that period of our marriage. Many interesting and unusual people lived there, some of whom were class mates of mine in medical school. A few vignettes might describe the tenor of life on Fourth Street.

Our landlord Gary S. was married to a young French bride who could not speak a word of English. They named their young son Willow, apparently from my perspective, to make the poor kid's future life miserable. Bob W., a medical student, suffered from manic episodes and his parents had him committed to inpatient psychiatric treatment on one occasion. They actually sent the "men in the white suits", an ambulance crew, who forcefully restrained Bob in a straight jacket and took him off in the middle of the day as we all watched, transfixed by our perplexity in this situation.

Doward N., living in the flat just below us, loved his gin straight up and often fell into a drunken slumber with the 45 recording of "Oh Donna" on the turntable, playing at maximum volume all night. Pastor B. lived across the street with his considerable family. His teenage daughter went to the emergency room one night with abdominal pain and delivered the cause of her pain in the obstetrical ward. Later, Clarence C., who lived across the street, asked Pastor B who the "lucky father" was. The reply was "never mind, it wasn't anything like that!" When Clarence went out on the porch of Pastor B's house and looked skyward, the Pastor asked what he was doing. Clarence said that "the last time this happened there was a star in the sky!" At that point Pastor B. chased Clarence across the street and angrily told him never to come back. Butch D. lived on the far end of the street. He and his friends had regular "swishing shows" where they dressed up in drag and performed. Kris was once invited to one of these "performances" when I was on call. Among other reactions, she was impressed at how expensive the clothing was for this affair.

Even my brother Mark lived with us for a short time and then moved across the street to an apartment building. We saw him often and he and Kris became good friends. Mark was just starting out with Ford Motor Company at that time.

As my schooling progressed, Kris and I continued our marital roles of medical student husband and teacher-provider wife. Kris was a good English teacher and was very attentive to her classes. Having a heavy class load, she always had papers to correct and sometimes I would help read and criticize the writing efforts of her students. Because she felt that her duty as an English teacher was to teach her students how to express themselves correctly in writing, she usually had a large volume of written assignments that required a significant amount of her time to read, digest and respond to with appropriate comment to the effort. Multiple choice tests, videos, workbooks and other less time consuming techniques were not part of her repertoire.

My own experience with clinical instructors was edifying as well. It is imperative to have mentors and role models to learn the aspects of medicine that do not reduce to book work. Medicine is still part science and part art. *Ars longa, vida brevis;* the art is long, and life is short, as the Latin saying goes. The Hippocratic Oath speaks of the student physician's need to respect "him who taught me this Art . . . by precept, lecture, and every other mode of instruction". I was fortunate to have many such good teachers in my clinical years and it is important to acknowledge some of them here.

One such fine physician, Anthony "Tony" Nolke, named the best teacher by our class, was recognized at our graduation ceremony in 1972. He was a Professor of Pediatrics, and worked out of Children's Hospital. We all had contact with Dr Nolke during our rotations through pediatrics. He was a masterful clinician who always had something unusual to impart. I remember being with a group of students on rounds at Children's when he asked a boy of eight to tell the young doctors about his five open heart surgeries. We were all amazed when this young patient precisely reeled off medical terms and procedures, with total recall of his history. When we gathered outside in the hall, Dr. Nolke asked us what we thought of him. We were all clearly impressed with his mastery of the details of his medical treatment. Tony pointed out the sobering fact that his precocity came at the expense of spending all his life in hospitals talking to adults. Obviously, he had not had a normal childhood and had not been able to interact with other children. The adult sounding speech was thus an unfortunate mark that he bore rather than a positive attribute

Vainutis Vitkevicius, M.D. is another physician who had a profound effect on my medical training. "Dr. Vee", as he was known to everyone, was the Chairman of the Department of Oncology. He was an immigrant from Lithuania and saw first hand the brutality of Soviet Communism. As a skilled clinician, his ability in physical diagnosis was exemplary. His knowledge in his field was broad and he was a tireless worker on behalf of patients. His bedside manner was uplifting for even the most serious of cancer patients, and he was certainly referred the most dire cases. To this day, he is still associated with the Karmanos Cancer Center in Detroit. They are fortunate to have had him all these years, as was I to have been a student in his tutelage.

Lastly there was Daniel Meyers, M.D., an old time clinician who worked in a number of interesting settings, including as a physician with the railroads. He had actually seen things such as Typhus epidemics, about which we could only read. He also had written, in conjunction with his brother Gordon Meyers, a textbook of internal medicine. On rounds, when expounding on patient care or medicine, he usually looked around at the group of students and residents. If he saw a medical student paging through a handbook, he just smiled and asked that student, "Is the book right?" This was not braggadocio on his part; rather, it was frankly true that Dr. Meyers was a better source than any book when it came to questions about medicine. He knew and respected Dr. Vee and he often argued skeptically about the cancer drugs that Vee prescribed. He always told him "Vee, if I get cancer I want Five Roses and not 5-FU". Another facet about this man was that he liked his drink after long days in the hospital. He was noted for his quote about alcoholism. He would ask the students on rounds, "What is the definition of an alcoholic?" After listening to several attempts to answer he said with his gravelly low voice, "The definition of an alcoholic is a patient that drinks more than his doctor". Peering over the rim of his glasses, he then added, "And I don't make the diagnosis too often!" Dan Meyers was a truly remarkable individual, a man of character, and a fine doctor. It was a privilege to have known him.

The clinical years are the time when most medical students determine what they will choose for their postgraduate specialty. Often, the rotations in the third year serve to sort out where the student's preferences lie. As my last two years drew to a close, I decided that general internal medicine was what I wanted to specialize in during my residency. I liked medicine because it involved the broad issues that we had studied in our years of medical course work. Medicine was the basis from which all other specialties grew, and as such, it appealed to me.

# CHAPTER 6

## LEFTIST POLITICS

As medical school progressed into the second and third year I became associated with a group of med students and several practicing physicians who volunteered their time to deliver "free" medical care several nights each week. Of course, health care is never really free since even when the service is donated, there is inevitably a cost for medications, supplies and the cost of the space allotted. This clinic was coordinated by a Black woman from the local community, Mrs. Lucille Wright. It was located in the basement of one of the buildings in the Jeffries Housing Project. This housing complex was one of those federally-funded, low-income projects which were not only generally crime ridden, but also plagued by inept management and abuse of the premises by some of the tenants. We attempted to get donated medications from pharmaceutical representatives as well as donated exam room equipment to facilitate the operation of the clinic. Unfortunately, we had access to only rudimentary lab work and x-ray studies were non-existent.

This "free medical care" idea was an outgrowth of the dictum that medical care was a "right" of every citizen and that the poor, in particular, should have "access" to care. It was also part of a politically motivated movement in medical schools and hospitals that was present in other places that we knew of, like Chicago and San Francisco. The premise of this effort seemed reasonable enough, since only an apparent philistine could disagree with the idea that health care was a "right" of the citizenry. By implication, those who objected to this statement were in favor of "denying" health care to the vulnerable. We also tended to gloss over the inconsistencies of the case that housing and food, which were much more basic to survival, were not posited as rights. The fact remained that if something was a right of one man then it became the duty of government to compel another to provide it[38]. The arrogance of thought that included health care as a "right" was largely a product of the fact that health care was the field in which we labored. Did our pious gathering consider health care more sacred than farming or carpentry? Perhaps we felt that we were doing God's work (although only a secular God would be acceptable) and that made such efforts more important and more politically significant.

The group of students that were involved with the Jeffries Clinic was to the left of the political spectrum, perhaps way to the left. I came into medical school with definite leftist leanings, which were based on my perceptions about the war, civil rights and other social issues, as I previously discussed. The left then, as now, considered itself the part of the political spectrum that belonged to the "intelligentsia" of the population. In those days, with the arrogance of youth, I had little reason for circumspection in regard to the self-described intellectual class. It would only be later in life and with greater maturity that I would begin to sense the agenda and the hubris of those who considered themselves part of that vanguard of the population at large. At that time, it just seemed natural and right that if the smart, enlightened people were on the left, then I also belonged on the political left. This led to my associations with others in and out of medical school who were involved with not only the Jeffries clinic but other societal issues as well.

Those of us with such common political perspectives and some who worked at the Jeffries clinic decided to form a "collective", to use a popular idiom of the day. Not all of us were aware of what this entity was or what it intended. I had some impression that it would afford a chance to discuss and study our clinic activity in a greater political perspective. For others, there might have been a different agenda. More than a few class mates and friends were part of this collective, but several whose names stand out to me were Howard "Howie" Beckman, Robert "Bobby" Frank, and Larry Leichman. Bobby's wife Sharon Popp and Larry's wife Gail also figured prominently in the group over the next few years. Bobby and Howie were from the Boston area, Larry and Gail from New York and Sharon Popp was from Detroit. The three guys were Jewish and considered Kris and I to be "Goyim", which of course, we were.

Getting to know these Easterners was an interesting process. My eye-opening summer in NYC and my four years at Michigan had not prepared me completely for the interaction. For one thing, they were more overtly political than any other people I had previously met. Almost any discussion had a political spin, particularly a left-leaning political spin to it. They were fun to be around because they were intelligent, funny, and possessed a cynical sense of humor. I enjoyed their friendship, even though at times I thought that they looked at me as an anomaly. After all, what did a Midwestern twenty-something from a generally conservative background see in the leftist leanings of these Eastern Jewish guys?

The cultural divide between us included ethnicity, but there were also non-ethnic factors. For example, Midwesterners like me were struck with the aggressive, competitive nature of those from the Eastern part of the U.S. It took me some time to find that this was only an initial impression and that after getting to know these guys, we were more alike than first suspected. The ethnic divide was often an object of humor as we became better acquainted. Bobby Frank, who was an entertaining story teller, related that his parents told him when growing up, "Don't worry about those Goyim and their sports and free time; just keep going to Hebrew school on Saturdays and one day they'll be working for you!"

Some thought the collective needed a name. Thus, we set out to find one. Actually, I think that it was more likely that some already knew what name they wanted to adopt, and presented their suggestion to the group for confirmation. I now know how that works because I have found that when raising kids, for example, it is sometimes better if an idea is presented in a way that they think they were the ones that thought of it. It is not always easy to do but, in this case, it was done masterfully. The collective was named after Norman Bethune, who was a Canadian surgeon and a member of the Canadian Communist Party who visited the Soviet Union in 1935. Joining the North Chinese Army in 1938, he went to the Shanxi-Hobei border region of China to deliver medical care. Within a year he became accidentally infected during surgery and died of septicemia.

Bethune was famous (infamous?) for being written about by Mao Tse-tung in his essay "In Memory of Norman Bethune"[39]. Now it was clear that none but the most dedicated lefties knew the slightest thing about Norman Bethune and his exploits, much less all the preceding information. In group dynamics it stands to reason that if some know in detail and others have not a clue, the game goes to those that know every time. Nevertheless, the name of this motley band of medical students and associates, for several years at least, was the "Norman Bethune Collective".

It was during this time of interaction with the collective that I first became acquainted with the term and the reality of "political correctness". Discussions of any nature had to be purged of any hint of the three "isms"; sexism, classism and racism. Those sufficiently unaware of the ground rules were often corrected or criticized by other discussants. Frequently, Sharon Popp served as a combination of parliamentarian and sergeant-at-arms in the rubric of Robert's Rules of Order. Her antenna was especially sensitive to comments that could be construed as male chauvinist or sexist in nature. In retrospect, such "discussions" were a sterile affair. Political correctness actually was a not so subtle technique to control the content of what was said during conversation and was a major impediment to truthful expression.

Because the group was made up chiefly of strong-willed and garrulous males, someone suggested that the smaller number of women in the crowd form their own "Women's Group". This was tried with mixed results. Some females objected to the idea that they should automatically imitate the larger collective just because others thought that necessary. Kris, as usual, had good instincts about this and was one who was unhappy with the form and the content of the women's group. She also objected to the attitude that was common then that women who chose to stay home and rear children were somehow less valuable in the eyes of the feminists of that day.

Much of what passed for political analysis came from a socialist and even communist perspective. It was most peculiar that these well-bred, well-educated young people, who obviously had benefited from American freedom and capitalism, analyzed the world's problems from an opposite dialectic. Inevitably, a free capitalist society like ours was automatically in the wrong. Marxist reasoning is a curious blend of untenable beliefs and a fervent messianic world view. For example, some in our collective subscribed to the belief that there would be a world wide revolution in which "people of color" would rise up and gain power over time. Convinced that this was the eventual course of history, the USA would obviously be on the wrong side of the trend and ergo, was in the wrong. There was really no way to discuss such beliefs as this since it amounted to a secular version of religiosity, which was not open to rational discourse. The Parousia of world revolution was to be led by those in the elite circles and in particular by a great leader. Perhaps some thought that great leader might be someone such as Lenin or Mao but there should have been enough of a dismal track record to disqualify them as candidates. It was a lesson in frustration to discuss politics with those that hold such a worldview.

Those who held to such an exegesis of the world situation had a hard time explaining it to others, at least with a straight face, and tended to let out such feelings only in the comfort of a small group of like-minded individuals. There was almost a "Jim Jones-Kool-Aid" character to such groups since they were by nature insulated from a colder realism about things that happened around them. There was the tendency to look at the greater society in terms of them and us. I don't want to over do this analysis, because most of the time the Norman Bethune Collective was involved in the Jeffries clinic or in a related food co-op at the farmer's market. Also, medical school alone took up the great majority of our time and that would only be exacerbated by residency. Nevertheless, the same undercurrent of unreality that existed in traditional Marxist dogma also existed in the "collective".

One curious topic to me was the talk of "armed struggle" and "necessary violence" by the far left[40]. In academic circles, the tendency was to speak of bloody purges and mass executions as something which was necessary for the forces of "the people" to succeed. This was true in the writings of John Paul Sarte from the 1930's and remains true in current screeds of someone like Noam Chomsky. Cushy academics spoke of such things from the comfort of their tenured sites in the ivy palaces. Theorists neither became the battle ready conscripts or the innocent bystanders of the wars that resulted from their ideas. The people who suffered the ill of these fevered dreams were those caught in the brutal flames of the conflagration that resulted from them. Some of the most nefarious Marxists fancied themselves thinkers as well as leaders. For example, Pol Pot was in Paris during his student years of the 1950's and attended the coffee houses of the socialists along the Seine[41]. When he returned to Cambodia he put into effect a regime more brutal than any before it and those who were the recipients of his utopian vision were murdered in numbers approaching 1,200,000. Mao Tse-tung, who had published the silly *Little Red Book* and other tracts, said that "Political power grows out of the barrel of a gun". He put that dictum into effect against millions of his own people during the Cultural Revolution and other debacles.

As if to show solidarity of thought or revolutionary fervor, some of my radical friends used various violent metaphors in discussing politics during the late 60's and early 70's. For instance, they said that people had to "fight" the police at demonstrations in order not to be intimidated and to show "solidarity". This type of talk was rich with irony for me. Having engaged in physical and demanding sports before, I had a hard time imagining these slightly built, non-martial, out-of-shape guys "fighting" anybody, especially not tough city cops and hardened military types. This tendency of leftists to engage in talk so far removed from reality was patently ridiculous. Even then I suspected that such talk was merely rhetorical flourish, but words have meanings and to throw them around so loosely made the speaker seem silly.

Perhaps the language of violence was no more of a ridiculous euphemism than many other things that Marx and his leftist heirs have said. To say that communism means "From each according to his abilities, to each according to his means" was poppycock in view of the means we now know were employed to bring about this unachievable platitude. To suggest that the necessary "dictatorship of the proletariat" would "wither away" was pure Pollyanna. The ghastly entity of the Soviet Union would no more "wither away" after the revolution than Rome would have freely opened her gates to the barbarians. When one thinks seriously about such things and applies common sense, it becomes risible that Marx would have the chutzpah to say that "religion is the opium of the people". *Au contraire*, what must he himself have been smoking?

Since the majority of the collective members were Jewish, and with appropriate deference to the inadequacy of ethnic profiling, I realized that more than a few American Jews have a disconcerting tendency for the facile acceptance of leftist politics. There are obvious and dramatic exceptions to such an assertion, such as Henry Kissinger the Secretary of State under Richard Nixon and Paul Wolfowitz, the Assistant Secretary of Defense under George Bush. There are also the eloquent writings and speeches of Norman Podhoretz and David Horowitz, who both in different ways broke with their leftist pasts.

However, back in my medical school and residency days, overwhelmingly, the young Jewish men and women that I met were reflexively liberal or radical. These same children of successful Jewish families, who had made good livings in our economy of market capitalism, were cynically critical of American capitalism as well as strongly anti-American with respect to our involvement in Southeast Asia. Moreover, they also criticized the domestic policies of our government with respect to the differences between the races, and with respect to disputes between labor and management. Often they demonstrated by their attitudes and lifestyles disrespect for traditional American values of accountability, sacrifice and acceptance of the rules of fair play. These are all things which their parents certainly must have taught them and which contributed to their personal success up until that point.

It was with particular puzzlement that I then began to learn of the position that my Jewish friends had toward the Israeli-Palestinian conflict. Here was a struggle where Jewish Americans should rally in support. After all, the tiny state of Israel had been attacked four times by the surrounding Arab countries, the most recent of which had just occurred in 1967. Israel was the only democratic country in the region, having been established with much blood and sweat, on the heels of the Holocaust. The Palestinians were relegated to refugee camps more because their Arab neighbors did not want to assimilate them and less because Israel took their lands. Israel, even at that time, was the recipient of frequent terrorist attacks. Its citizens lived in a state of siege. This situation called for support, at the very least, from American Jews and moreover, from their American government.

Unfortunately, the Palestinian cause became a *cause celebre* of the radical left. Like good party members, my left-leaning Jewish friends turned away from the defense of their historic homeland. They made up rationalizations about "Zionism" being the problem with Israel and signed on to the irredentist claims of the Palestinians and the left. Here again, I give credit to my level-headed wife. She was even more troubled about this aspect of leftist deception than was I. Her support of the Israeli cause went back to her college days when her reading of "Exodus" by Leon

Uris, and other books, sensitized her to Israel's plight. She did
not accept this double-talk explanation that the Jews were guilty
of Zionism and thus presumably should be pushed into the sea
for their sins against the perennially poor Palestinians. Kris saw
much earlier than I that the terrorist actions of the Palestinians
disqualified them from the support of reasonable people. Their
subsequent devolution to strapping bombs on twelve year olds
and detonating them at someone's wedding in Tel Aviv was the
logical outcome of such evil treachery. That tyrants would support
such acts with payments of "blood money" to the families of these
children is even more despicable.

Moses may well have had his problems with the wayward
and "stiffnecked people"[42] of the tribes of ancient Israel but the
modern day apostasy of many Jews is the glib acceptance of the
tenets of the anti-Israel, anti-American left. There is no moral
equivalence between the terror of Hamas and the defense of the
Jewish homeland by the Israeli Army. With the recent return of
anti-Semitism across Europe, America and American Jewry must
not abandon Israel in her hour of need.

My sojourn to the left of the political spectrum was halted in
its tracks when I attended a meeting one night in the early 1970's.
I was asked to come to a study group meeting with some of my
friends from the collective. There were other people there as well
but the number consisted of less than a dozen individuals.
Although this group had been meeting for several weeks, this
was my first time in attendance. The subject of study was selected
writings of Vladimir Ilyich Ulyanov, also known as V.I. Lenin.
They all had copies of the book being discussed, I did not. I had
not previously known much about or read much about Lenin
and I had not read the writings to be discussed. I knew enough
to be suspicious of what I would subsequently hear that night.
The written polemics of this man and the reactions from those
assembled had as little relation to reality as I could imagine. As
I listened, the comments became harder and harder to tolerate. I
was like the delusional alcoholic suddenly brought back to reality
by a cold glass of water thrown across my face. The tableau of

that evening resonates in my memory. From that point on, although I harbored no animus to them, I knew that I would no longer share the utopian dreams and the other delusions of my leftist friends. My own journey took a turn.

Only later on did I learn of the extent of the crimes of V.I. Lenin. I learned of his psychopathic will to power, his heartless executions of anyone who stood in his way and the purges of his friends and associates. Author Mona Charon has written a book, published in 2003, and called *Useful Idiots*[43]. It's title comes from a phrase attributed to Lenin that described the part that self-deluded intellectuals from Western Democracies played in support of the communist world revolution. By rationalization, cover up and sheer naiveté these dupes acted as unwitting or even conscious smokescreens for what the state needed to accomplish to achieve power. To wit, the "necessary violence" and other forms of atrocity were much easier undertaken if the intelligentsia of the West kept outside sentiment in confusion. There in Detroit, at that study group meeting, was a sterling example of those "useful idiots" waving and reading from the text of the very man who considered them to be fools. That I was there at such a discussion of that sociopathic mass murderer is something that I regret and is a testament to the foibles of a youthful mind.

I also realized that the friendships of those on the left were very dependant on common political outlook. If one stops sharing a similar world view it became difficult for his other friends to continue on that friendship any longer. Aristotle, in the fourth century B.C., wrote that friendships were of three types[44]. First, the "friendships of convenience", in which, for example, someone may have worked with another and it was better or easier to be friendly than not. Then come the "friendships of pleasure"; here the friendship was based on a mutually shared activity or pursuit. Lastly, are the "friendships of character" where there is a mutual interest in getting to know the other person out of respect for whom and what that person is.

The friendships that Kris and I had with our friends from this era were of the second type of Aristotelian friendships. Once the shared political vision was gone there was little interest in keeping close from their standpoint and probably from ours as well. To have maintained our closeness would have required the interest of a friendship of character, and Aristotle correctly predicted that there are very few of these in a person's life. As a result, I have had little contact or only superficial contact with our friends from that time. While I do not know whether they have changed their views over time, I doubt that they have.

The youthful idealism that led me to such things as the Jeffries Clinic also led me to question many things about American society. Insofar as the medical clinic work was concerned, I feel that something positive came out of those efforts. How much benefit accrued to me or to others was not clear, and it would be prudent to be sanguine in my retrospective judgment. The people who were served received a benefit that was considerably less than could be expected if ancillary services were available. The help we rendered was finite with regard to clinic hours each week. Clinic operation lasted only several years before terminated by lack of continued availability of practitioners. The overall contribution to the long term medical needs of its patients was therefore, limited. I hope our involvement at Jeffries was not merely a Pyrrhic effort that did nothing but assuage our own vanity.

While the political involvements were in many ways misguided, in a greater sense they provided a personal learning experience for me and also for Kris. We helped each other through those times and continue to do so today. In our marriage, the pattern has been of mutual, not separate growth. In the process, indeed we have become friends of character to each other. For obvious reasons, we both knowingly enjoy the quote attributed to Winston Churchill; "Any man under thirty who is not a liberal has no heart, and any man over thirty who is not a conservative has no brains"[45]

# CHAPTER 7

## RESIDENCY AND FIRST BIRTHS

E very physician will testify that residency, and in particular that first year of residency following medical graduation, known as internship, was where the true test of adequacy occurred in medical training. The graduate knew the names and the progression of diseases, how to examine a patient, where to go to research a patient problem, but now he was called on to take responsibility for the care of sick patients. His decisions were held up to scrutiny by his medical mentors and his peers. The burden of accountability for good or ill devolved to him as a medical doctor and as a person.

A medical student was protected from the full burden of obligation to patients by layers of interns, residents and attending physicians. During the third and fourth year rotations, even though exposed to critical decisions regarding patients, the student was not primarily responsible for these decisions or for carrying them out. When residency started there was a whole new dimension to the name "doctor" which was not realized completely before. The first year resident fitted into a pecking order of sorts, a chain of command, which gave him backup for front-line problems. But assessments that had to be made late at night or in the wee hours of the morning could not await the academic investigations and discussions of the next day.

One of the critical aspects that made the job of intern and resident so mentally challenging was the sheer number of hours that were worked. The call schedule at the time of my residency was generally every fourth night and on some rotations every third. The resident had to be physically "in house" during "night call", and frequently worked with little sleep. More recent studies having to do with the effects sleep deprivation suggest that it might lead to poor medical judgments and harmful patient care. I did not witness overt harm to patients from lack of sleep. However, unquestionably such deprivation did result in a tangible level of fatigue in the sleep deprived individual.

On many occasions, I stayed up all night with patient care and then tried to function for the rest of the next day until evening rounds were completed around 6 PM. I vividly remember being on morning rounds outside of the coronary unit (CCU) after one of my nights on call. While another resident was presenting the next case to the attending physician, I dozed off for just a moment while leaning against the wall, actually sleeping while standing bolt upright. When the seductive sleep sirens beckoned, there was no resistance from this tired intern. Dragging myself home after the long day following a night of work, I frequently fell asleep as my head hit the pillow; in only a few hours I was on my way back to the hospital for morning rounds.

Many careers required long hours of hard work. However, medicine was one of the few that required its acolytes to function on a regular basis while training, without sleep during the normal hours of sleep. Many critics contended that this was a silly convention and only retained by the residency program chiefs because they themselves went through the same requirement. These critics, some of whom were physicians themselves, characterized these call schedules as something similar to a fraternity hazing which was part of the initiation rights of membership. Concerned about the supposed harm to patients and to the residents, they called for significant reform or abolition of call. Having now seen the demands of patient care from years of practice, I know of the physician's need to act on behalf of patients in spite of sleeplessness and fatigue. Therefore, reform of resident night call should proceed prudently and it should not be radically altered; the traditional system still has valuable lessons to impart to the doctor in training.

That said, it is still entertaining to look back on those sleepless years of residency and reflect on its effect on our marriage and social life. Living within modest means, our social interactions were not exorbitant. Kris and I took in occasional movies and every so often got together with other residents to talk, eat and drink some beer. Inevitably, before the end of the evening, those of us who had been recently on call fell asleep in various positions. Sometimes sleep overtook us in the midst of conversation, sometimes while sitting propped against the wall. The level of tiredness was such that social functions frequently left something to be desired. These effects were more prominent during the first year or two of residency and improved in the later years as the schedules became less onerous and we were less sleep deprived.

Officially, my residency position was part of the Wayne State University Affiliated Internal Medicine Program, which included many different metropolitan hospitals. My base hospital was Detroit General Hospital. The first year of medical residency allowed several months of elective rotation, so within these limits, I attempted to set up the year similar to an old style rotating internship. I wanted to broaden the background of my training experience to include more than traditional internal medicine. Thus, I took the opportunity to spend two months at Children's Hospital, where I gained invaluable experience in the care of critically ill pediatric patients as well as an assignment to the pediatric outpatient clinic. In-patient pediatrics is a different species of care than well baby visits, especially at Children's Hospital, where some of the most tragic and heart-rending in-patient cases were referred. I found that children could rapidly become deathly ill. They could mend and heal just as fast. One of my most memorable patients was Keisha, a beautiful three year old girl with a fatal case of leukemia. Perhaps it now sounds as an unsuitable tribute, but I later named my German Shepherd

Keisha, the dog given to me by my brother Clyde and the only dog I have ever owned and loved.

I also elected to spend time on a special surgical rotation known as "E-Surg". This emergency surgical rotation was located right at Detroit General Hospital. It was an intense experience requiring "call" on every third night. The E-Surg residents were busy night and day with acute surgical emergency patients, cases that were often the handiwork of the violent inner city specialty we dubbed "the knife and gun club". In cases of gun shot wounds (GSW) to the abdomen, it was instructive to scrub into the OR and find how many structures could be injured from even one projectile as it traversed the viscera. The few hours of sleep we procured as we shuttled back and forth from the emergency room to the operating room, usually took place on a spare gurney in the hallway off the surgical ward. It was unusual even then for a medical resident to take a surgical rotation since an academic chasm existed between these competing specialties. This was analogous to different branches of the armed services where, for example, it would be unusual for an army recruit to spend time aboard an aircraft carrier. In retrospect, the experience in E-Surg, like the time in peds, were valuable assets for my future medical practice.

The old Detroit General[46] was a throw back to the days of large patient wards. Although there were isolation rooms, there were not private rooms per se. One ward was a lock-up prison ward where a city police guard unlocked the entrance for us to make rounds and to provide patient care. The regular medical and surgical wards were spacious, with high ceilings, and held somewhere between six and twelve patient beds. Because many of the inner city patients had haphazard outpatient care, their problems were often far advanced when they were hospitalized with acute medical conditions. While adding to the acuity of care, this also provided a unique learning experience for the medical and surgical residents at Detroit General.

As a resident in internal medicine I was assigned to the wards, the clinics and to the emergency room at various times. The emergency room of DGH was a zoo of every species of acute and chronic diseases, and the overflow on weekends made some of the current TV sitcoms look tame by comparison. Often, the line of gurneys with patients on them awaiting X-rays backed way down the hallways. X-ray studies for patients with more emergent conditions always took priority, meaning that the wait for non-emergent films could be interminable. Once, I saw an agitated, drug crazed prisoner in that line who, while chained to his gurney, rocked it over onto the floor, pinning his arm under it as it fell, shattering his humerus. This unfortunate fellow was obviously so high that the full impact of his painful angulated arm was not as severe as it would have been in a more sober state. Acutely psychotic patients were often lined up waiting for psych consultation for days at a time. The cacophony of their babblings added to the surreal din of the emergency room. Dante, in his travels through *Purgatorio*, might well have been describing scenes like this.

In addition to the rich clinical experience available when training in an inner city hospital, there were down sides as well. A chronic shortage of medical supplies and simple things like sheets and gowns existed, something attributable to the bureaucracy of city governance, under which DGH fell. Because of these factors it sometimes seemed that we were practicing in a third world country and not in the technologically advanced US. With less oversight from senior staff physicians than at some of the private suburban hospitals, more responsibility fell on the residents for making medical decisions and carrying them out. Pressures to triage treatment frequently arose, using time and resources for patients with greater hope of recovery and with less end-stage medical problems. A need to arrange priority and necessity of patient care has always existed, but the need was more acute there at DGH.

For example, the chronic shortage of ventilators led to using the available ones for some patients rather than for others. In optimal situations, the level of aggressiveness of this form of medical care was discussed with relatives, spouses and significant others. Often, in the inner city, none were present to speak for the single, destitute men that we saw and the care was thus left to the residents and staff to decide. As a young physician, some of my decisions that were made there under those circumstances were rashly considered and are bothersome to me still.

Residency was the first time where I was paid during my training, in contradistinction to the years of undergraduate and medical school work, where the money went in the opposite direction in the form of tuition. It is amusing to look back on these first years of medical residency and to contemplate the remuneration that we received. As an intern at DGH, my salary for the year was less than $9000. This seemed reasonable at the time, since only a few years before that, in 1969, the first year residents were making only $6000 per year[47]. We often joked about how much we were getting paid, given our regular long hours plus the night and weekend call schedule. In a good week the hourly rate was between $1.30 and $1.50. Nevertheless, from the financial standpoint, to my school teacher wife and me, the first year of training was somewhat like easy street. After years of payments and loans, the resident's stipend was a welcome reprieve. Between her modest teaching salary and my own, and with very little fixed expense to pay, we had a financial freedom that was unrestricted, even by our present day circumstances. In contrast, it is most amusing to note that present day residents in the post graduate year one (PGY-I) of the Detroit Medical Center Internal Medicine Program are paid a salary of $38,850. Benefits include such things as medical/dental care, life insurance policies, etc[48]. Even taking inflation into account, that is quite a difference.

Many colorful anecdotes occurred to me while I was a medical resident. In my second year, while assigned to the emergency room at Detroit General, the chief resident asked me to allow a reporter from The Detroit Free Press to accompany me as I worked. This young woman, the medical writer for her paper, was assigned to do a story on the city hospital and what the typical resident would encounter at such a busy place. In the weekend pandemonium of the ER, I was evaluating a feverish and confused alcoholic patient. The reporter was interested in seeing just what the workup of such a patient would entail.

At this point, a lumbar puncture (spinal tap) to rule out meningitis was required in this patient, and the reporter was eager to observe. The man was febrile and delirious and would not object to her presence. After the nurse quickly arranged the spinal tray, we pulled the curtains around the gurney in the room. The nurse helped me to position the patient on his side and held him in the proper position so he did not move, while the reporter stood at the head of the gurney. I explained each step of the procedure, while prepping, draping and freezing the site on the patient's lower back, occasionally glancing at the reporter, who was taking notes. Just as I inserted the spinal needle and noted the return of clear spinal fluid into the collection tubes, I again glanced at the young reporter. This time I immediately saw that she was no longer writing, now appearing quite pale and sweaty. In a moment she began to wobble and started to fall. Reaching my free gloved hand over I grabbed her arm and was able to help her to a chair. The nurse then helped me re-glove the contaminated hand. I finished the procedure while the reporter slowly came around from her simple faint. Needless to say, she did not feel like staying around for more activity in the ER that night. Instead, she thanked us and left for home. That episode constituted my entire professional contact with the media during my residency and, since then as well. Feeling that I acquitted myself admirably, I have no aspirations for further exposure.

In my second year of medical residency something happened which changed my perspective on life and altered my own goals profoundly. That event was the birth of my daughter Erika. When Kris told me earlier in the year that she had tested positive for pregnancy, we both looked forward with happy expectation. We wanted a more suitable place to have our child and found a nice home on the East Side of Detroit on Devonshire Street, just off of Chandler Park Drive. In this new phase of our lives, we decided that our days on Fourth St. were over. The new neighborhood was populated by many Detroit Police and Fire employees and it was one of the last areas on the East Side that had not been transformed from all white to all black residents.

At that time in Detroit, there was very little integration in housing in any of the neighborhoods. After Brown vs. The Board of Education in 1954, The Civil Rights Act of 1960, and the bussing orders of the 1960's and 1970's, little evidence remained that blacks and whites could or would live together. Then as now, race remained as one of America's chief problems searching for solution. We did not move to solve that problem but to give us more room and freedom to raise our first child. The home was brick Tudor in style, in good structural shape, had a small yard and a one car garage in the back. The neighborhood was busy but seemed generally safe.

Our daughter Erika was born at Hutzel Hospital on October 14, 1973, just one day after Kris' 26th birthday. Our German Shepherd Keisha was troubled at first that this new bundle we brought home displaced her from the position of being our only "child", but over time Keisha and Erika became best of friends. It was interesting that Keisha always sat right outside of Erika's bedroom on the second floor when any strangers or the rare babysitters came into the house. When Erika was older and able to play in the back yard, it was reassuring that Keisha would stay right with her all the time.

As the first born and the focus of our attention, we endeavored to do everything right for Erika. Under our tutelage, she had the best eating habits of any toddler that any of our friends or family had ever seen. She ate vegetables, yogurt, and even cooked mushrooms without complaint. She was a model child, her mother and father were so proud of her then. When Erika was almost three, our neighborhood threw a block party. A piñata was broken by the children present and the confectionary contents released. The other children began to play games, but Erika was busy gathering the candy from the piñata. She then sat on the stoop of the house and stuffed candy and chocolate into her mouth with both hands. Our little daughter, who had been raised on healthy foods, had discovered the carnal knowledge of candy! She had fallen out of the dietary Garden of Eden.

Residency in the third postgraduate year continued to be rigorous, but the time commitment was reduced, which allowed me to spend more time at home with my wife and daughter. Erika's birth started a reassessment of my personal and career goals. Although I had always envisioned myself primarily involved in clinical medicine and patient care, I had also entertained the possibility of staying in academic medicine. As my training progressed however, I became more disenchanted with what I saw of medical academia, so I began to look more seriously at the possibility of primary care practice. At the same time that my role in family life took on more than just nominal consequence, Kris decided that she did not want to raise kids in a big city. We considered whether a small town or suburban medical practice might be plausible. Having become more familiar with Kris' home town of Iron Mountain and knowing that they needed an internist, the prospect of practice there was increasingly appealing.

After three years of medical residency, most residents went into sub-specialty fellowships or into practice. Since I was considering practice in Iron Mountain, where there was little specialty backup closer than one hundred miles, it was wise to take an additional year of training. In my fourth post-graduate year I planned to take additional training in cardiology, rheumatology, gastroenterology and oncology. During the rotations of that year I also studied assiduously for my internal medicine boards, which were scheduled to be given in the spring of 1976.

As a senior resident, with less strain of overnight call, I devoted myself to preparation for the board exam. After my day at the assigned hospitals I walked over to the Wayne Medical Library (The Schiffman Library) to study almost every evening. I usually took a small bag dinner with me and after eating it in the study cells of the library, I often put my head down for a twenty minute power nap. Reinvigorated, I spent the next few hours studying, until about 10 or 11 PM. At that point, I drove back to our home on the East Side, only to get ready to repeat the same process the next day. Within the residency programs, the Internal Medicine Board Exam had the reputation for being academically tough and the failure rate was said to be one third. For this exam I put forth one year of study. It was the longest and the most arduous preparation of all that I had undertaken.

Kris became pregnant with our second child in the fall of 1975. To put this all in perspective with my family life, her due date was in the vicinity of my board exam, but I never entertained the possibility that the two events would end up in conflict. The two-day exam was scheduled to take place in downtown Detroit on the 15th and the 16th of June, 1976. With about six weeks to go on my study schedule and with a very pregnant wife who showed no signs of labor, I began to have that sinking feeling. The exam and the due date were drawing near by the day. Even though Kris told me that she would do fine without me, I dearly wanted to be with her when she delivered. The only thing I wanted less than missing the birth of my second child was spending another year studying for the medical boards.

On the morning of June 15th I kissed Kris good bye, and told her to call the exam location if she went into labor. I did the same thing as I left on the 16th. Miraculously, I completed the exam without a call. As if by Divine intervention, early on the morning of June 17th Kris' water broke, so we quickly drove to Hutzel Hospital, where she delivered my first son, Stephen Gabriel Leonard. At that inner-city hospital, he was the only white baby in the nursery that day. However, at 9 pounds, 11 ounces, he was the biggest. I am grateful to Gabe for many things, but first among them was his wonderful timing in coming to us the day just after my exam was completed. In the fall of that year, I was notified that my year of study was successful. I was certified as a diplomat of the American Board of Internal Medicine.

My residency experience prepared me well for my intended primary care practice. Having just taken my board exam, I felt current and capable. I was eager to see my own patients and manage their medical problems. I felt confident to do so. From a business standpoint, I had little knowledge of what was proper procedure in setting up a practice. That was not a subject that was covered in training. Even at that time, it was more common for young doctors to work for a larger organization or group practice. A truly solo practitioner was uncommon in 1976. Nevertheless, everything was headed in the right direction, with no problem on the horizon that could not be conquered. We sold the home in Detroit and moved our family North to the Upper Peninsula.

# CHAPTER 8

## THE MOVE TO IRON MOUNTAIN

A new phase of life awaited Kris and me as we drove to her home town of Iron Mountain in June of 1976. She drove the fully packed Chevy Nova with Erika and her newborn brother Gabe while I drove the rental panel truck with all our modest belongings. These belongings were so "modest" that "Howie" Beckman, a fellow medical resident who helped me load our furniture in the van, suggested jokingly that we should "throw all this junk out and buy some new stuff when we get there". He was right about the furnishings but we were in no position to do so at that time. We had been fortunate to find a great old home at 102 Pine Street in Iron Mountain. We were financially stretched with loans for the initial costs to open my practice. This crush was in addition to the accumulated student loans dating back past medical school to my undergraduate days. We had to make do with the old "stuff".

In spite of all that debt and expense, up to that point, we were never as happy as when we moved our young family into what was formerly known as the "Kingsford Home". This was named for the then deceased Ted and Winnie Kingsford, members of the family homonymous of the town of the same name. Kingsford and Iron Mountain were twin cities divided by a single street, with a total population of about 15,000 souls, as it also is now. Our new home was a two-story, wood-sided white home, set on a roomy lot which had a small stream running through a ravine behind it. It was in a safe, quiet neighborhood; a perfect place for kids to grow up.

The start-up date for my new medical practice was August 2nd. I worked out of the Medical Park Clinic, eventually becoming a business partner with the other doctors there. Kris' mother Muriel helped in setting up office procedures, interviewing employees and getting new patients scheduled ahead of time. This meant that my practice was almost as busy as we could manage from the start, rather than going through a period of stagnancy until the volume increased.

In addition, Ray Leonard was doing what he could in town to spread the news. My Dad and Mom had come up for a visit and in no time my Dad, in his own inimitable way, had visited several of the local pharmacists, informing them that his son was starting a medical practice in town. I was surprised to find out later, when speaking to these pharmacists by phone, that they already had been made aware of me by such introductions.

The hospital where I applied for privileges was Dickinson County Memorial Hospital. There was also a Veterans Hospital in Iron Mountain, but they had their own staff and there was only limited professional interaction between the two. At that time, Dickinson was primarily an inpatient facility which had 120 beds. The entire medical staff numbered 18 Physicians. This included two general surgeons, two orthopedic surgeons, two pathologists, two radiologists, a gynecologist, an oral surgeon, a urologist and a larger contingent of general and family practitioners. The hospital then, as now, was run by an administrator who was overseen by a board appointed by the county board of commissioners and who served terms of four years per appointment. The board was very receptive to new ideas and requirements with regard to my specialty, which was new to their facility. They were eager to develop an intensive care unit, so they accommodated, when it was necessary, to purchase the monitoring equipment which was needed to operate that unit. I held classes for the nursing staff to train them in intensive care issues, including cardiac monitoring and arrhythmia recognition. All in all, the chance to develop a medical unit from the ground up was very gratifying for me as a new physician. It was also an important contribution to health care in our local area.

Looking back on those days when our small county hospital had limited specialty availability provides considerable contrast with our situation today. We labored to do well with what we had to offer. The philosophy was that what services we offered should meet the same standard as any hospital providing the same care. We often needed to send patients one hundred miles to the North or South, at a minimum, for tertiary care and other services that we did not have locally. But, in spite of the more recent construction of a new, expanded facility and with considerable expansion of medical staff, we still properly send those patients out for services not present at Dickinson. Remarkably, the present day medical staff of Dickinson County Hospital has grown to 73 active staff, with 27 consulting staff physicians, reducing greatly the need to refer out for non-existing services. Furthermore, the hospital stands as the county's largest employer, with 771 employees[49]. There has been exceptional growth in a score and one half years.

The early years of my practice were a satisfying experience for me. As I came to know my patients over time I developed a friendship with many of them. Because of the mortal nature of my specialty of adult medical care, many of my patients were older, suffering from the diseases of degeneration and aging. Many fine individuals I have known have passed on, having taught me the lesson that even modern medicine with all its discoveries cannot change the basic conditions that determine human destiny. I knew this fact as a student and resident but in my own practice I came to understand it more comprehensively. The doctor can aid and comfort, but not often save his patients from the immutable course of many of the afflictions of our nature. With the help of my patients, I have become wiser in the proper use of our technology. I recognize wisely when technology merely becomes a ruse for ineptitude.

The happiness I felt with my new medical practice and with the new home for our family was contrasted by the regrettable events in the nation and the world at large. Our country was still smarting from the extrication of American Military forces from Vietnam in 1973, which led to a murderous takeover of South Vietnam by the North Vietnamese in 1975. Neighboring Cambodia was ravaged by the maniacal Pol Pot in the years of 1975-1979. His radical communist regime prematurely ended the lives of 1.2 million of its citizens. The resignation of Richard Nixon over the Watergate Scandal in 1974 was abetted and cheered by his enemies in the press, who also painted a generally gloomy scenario for the future of the United States.

Watergate was referred to by pundits as a "second-rate burglary", which occurred during the election campaign of 1972. The complicity of the executive branch was compounded by an inept cover up, an idiotic, indiscriminate recording of white house conversations and stonewalling by the president. These were accompanied by a press investigation and a relentless media drumbeat led by the Washington Post. The resignation of Nixon has been termed a "media *putsch*" by subsequent commentators[50]. If the same drumbeat had been directed against William Jefferson Clinton during his impeachment hearings in 1998, it might have resulted in his resignation as well.

The brief tenure of President Gerald Ford was obscured by continued grumbling from the left and criticism from them regarding Ford's pardon of Nixon. The fact that he made the decision to put the controversy to rest and to salve the national wounds was lost on these people. In a lackluster campaign against Ford in 1976, the election of Jimmy Carter portended more *Sturm und Drang* for the American electorate. Carter's presidency was overshadowed by rising interest rates, jumps in the price of gasoline and by events that unfolded in the Middle East in the country of Iran.

The so called "energy crisis" resulted in several presidential addresses to the nation. In July, 1979, Carter spoke of a "crisis of confidence . . . The erosion of our confidence in the future is threatening to destroy the social and the political fabric of America." Several days later he talked of "a national malaise" that was present in the country[51]. Also in the same year, the Soviet Union invaded Afghanistan, the same Soviet Union that the Carter state department had handled in the outdated and deferential method of *Détente* His response, in part, was to charge that Leonid Brezhnev had lied to him. In view of the Vietnam debacle, the state of the economy and our failing foreign policy, many surmised that the malaise of the country was perhaps related to leadership or lack thereof. The subsequent situation in Iran became the *coup de grace* of the Carter presidency.

The ailing Shah Pahlavi of Iran, the head of the longest running empire in history (the Persian Empire), was deposed by unrest among Shiite Muslims in that land. They seized power in 1979 and brought out of exile a radical cleric named Ayatollah Khomeini, installing him as their new leader. In retrospect, we can now look back on this event as an early warning to us of the rise of radical Islamic fundamentalism that would continue to plague the West until the present day. In November of that year, a group of 3000 students stormed the American Embassy and took sixty-six people hostage in the name of The Ayatollah. Thus began the "Iranian Hostage Crisis" which would follow Carter through the rest of his one term presidency[52].

The daily images of our blindfolded American hostages and the noisy mobs of delirious Iranians in Tehran chanting "Death to America, Death to Carter, Death to the Shah" counter posed with the growing, quiet rage of our citizenry who watched these happenings on their television screens. Yellow ribbons were hung on trees and posts outside homes around the United States and calls for action were sounded from many quarters. Americans were ready to support the president in what ever course he took. Unfortunately, the single military action did not occur until April, 1980, and that was an aborted rescue attempt involving eight helicopters launched from the aircraft carrier U.S. Nimitz in the Arabian Sea. Flying in a desert sandstorm and having mechanical troubles, two helicopters crashed and eight servicemen were killed. Four additional helicopters were abandoned and the survivors left the dead in the flames of the wreckage. President

Carter went into hiding during this time period, spending his time in a "Rose Garden" strategy and limiting his public appearances. Increasingly, he appeared impotent in the face of this crisis. Impatience grew in the public mind.

The presidential election of 1980 was a time when the people of our country saw clear differences in the candidates. They were ready to throw off the malaise that was said to encumber them. Perhaps it was unfair that the failure to resolve the hostage crisis was blamed on Jimmy Carter, since short of a declaration of war, there might not have been another alternative available. The hostages were, in fact, freed just after the election but while Carter was still the acting president. Prompted by the possibility that the new president might not act as favorably toward them as his predecessor, the Khomeini government quickly negotiated a deal for hostage release.

To more accurately assess his place in our political landscape, it is also noteworthy to review the actions of Jimmy Carter since his presidency. His association with Habitat for Humanity is cited frequently in the press, and although genuine, his public legacy includes more than hammering nails into 2X4's. Because of his efforts to promote peace in various areas of the world, he was recognized by the five member Norwegian Nobel Committee and awarded the Nobel Peace Prize for 2002. It is doubtful that those efforts have had much long term effect when one considers the current state of affairs in Haiti and North Korea, two of the places where he had been, in the words of the presenters, "seeking peaceful solutions and promoting social and economic justice."

Of greater concern to many citizens of the United States is the fact that the head of the Nobel Committee clearly signaled that they intended to send a political message to President Bush by this choice. "With the position Carter has taken on this, it can and must also be seen as criticism of the line the current U.S. administration has taken on Iraq", said Gunnar Berge[53]. This frank admission thus tainted the award itself and many asked whether Carter should have refused to accept it. But he did accept it, without any mention of these anti-American aspects.

Emblematic of this, the whole subject of the Nobel Peace Prize has been so politically tainted in the latter half of the 20th century that even nefarious people like Yasser Arafat can win such recognition. To me, the average US Marine with an M-16 does more for "peace" than all these preening candidates.

Later in the same year, Carter publicly called for America "to reduce and enforce the [international] agreement to eliminate chemical weapons, and the same way with nuclear weapons". In addition to calling for American disarmament, he further admonished his country with the statement, "There is a sense that the United States has become too arrogant, too dominant, too self-centered, proud of our wealth, believing that we deserve to be the richest and most powerful and influential nation in the world"[54].

It is with amazement and breathlessness that I read these words spoken by a former president of this great land. It is a credit to the American public that they were prescient enough to usher this man out of office in 1980 in favor of a man of faith and optimism in the American experiment. Ronald Reagan gave hope to a public that had enough of the defeatism and self-flagellation of the 1970's. His statement that it was "Morning in America" resonated in our country. His positive approach and persistent defense of America as a "City on a Hill" made Americans proud once again[55].

As president, Reagan faced the economic threat of inflation with tax cuts that brought a sustained recovery that stretched out over the next 20 years. He faced the Cold War threat of the Soviet Union and its communist minions with firmness. Against the carping of his critics and even the advice of his staff, he publicly called it an "Evil Empire". He rejuvenated the military with new weapons, some of which, like the B-1 Bomber, had been vetoed by Carter. He also raised military pay at all levels and made our men and women in service feel proud as well.

Reagan won his second term in 1984. He proved fearless in the cause of reducing Cold War tensions; negotiating arms control agreements while insisting that any agreement had to have parity to work. This meant that the excess of Soviet nuclear weapons had to be reduced in exchange for the (planned) deployment of the Pershing Missiles in Europe. When the Russians objected, he went ahead with the scheduled deployment. Thereby, he emphasized that there would be "peace through strength" and not just on a peace of paper. According to his philosophy, agreements had to have a reliable method for verification. His slogan "trust but verify" was well known. If an agreement did not have these qualities, then Reagan was prepared to walk away from it. Soviet leader Gorbachev learned this lesson unmistakably at the Reykjavik summit in 1986. He had been pressuring Reagan to abandon the Strategic Defense Initiative (SDI) as part of the settlement, but Reagan held firm. When Gorbachev said that it was "non-negotiable" Reagan simply closed his briefcase and went home. It was only a year later that Gorbachev reconsidered and traveled to Washington to sign the INF treaty. For the first time, this agreement eliminated an entire class of intermediate range missiles, complete with on-site inspections, a demand which had been resisted in the past.

Throughout his presidency Reagan accomplished his political objectives with cheerfulness and warmth, exuding optimism for the future. He did this with a steady raft of criticism and mean spirited comments from many in the "chattering class". Condescendingly, the intelligentsia felt Reagan was a light weight who had no experience in foreign policy and little understanding of the economy. Clark Clifford, the former Secretary of Defense under Johnson and career diplomat, called him an "amiable dunce", hardly a diplomatic statement from someone who was so skilled at the language of nuance. Even his supporters and White House staff were critical of him. There was serious disagreement about the use of the term "Evil Empire" and the arms control experts all thought Reagan would be bested by wily individuals like Gorbachev[56].

In another light, even the direst circumstances were sometimes met by the president with a sense of humor. The most notable example was when he was shot by John Hinkley in 1981.

As he arrived at the hospital with a .22 cal bullet lodged near his heart, he said to all the doctors, "Please tell me you're Republicans". Indeed, Reagan was enigmatic to many and received despicably by others, but to most of the "unwashed" out in the country, he was a welcome change in leadership and just what they needed after the decade of the 70's.

The common people of my new home town, the *volksgruppen* of Iron Mountain, liked Ronald Reagan. The president validated their patriotism and their aspirations regarding family and country. This was a great contrast to the "opinion-makers" in the intelligentsia, who denigrated him repeatedly. The malice and rancor exhibited toward him appeared petty and cheap and I wanted nothing of it. Increasingly, I found myself alienated from the self-described elite and drawn to the view of the plebeian locals.

Kris was pregnant with our third child, due in the spring of 1979. She delivered our second son, Zachary Charles Leonard on April 12th, fully one month post mature of his due date. He weighed 10 lbs. 11 oz. and actually appeared to be a month old from staying *en utero* so long. When they placed him on his belly to weigh him, he pushed himself up on the scale and looked curiously all around the delivery room. One of the physicians on our medical staff joked the next day that he saw Zach down in the hospital cafeteria smoking a cigar! This was the last pregnancy for Kris.

The purchase of a cottage on the Spread Eagle chain of lakes just across the state line in Wisconsin represented another significant aspect of our young family life. Spread Eagle was a special place for Kris, where her family had rented a small cottage for several weeks almost every year when she was young. As soon as I saw it, I became equally enthralled with that unique chain of lakes. We remained alert for any possible available places on those lakes and asked Kris' brother Chuck to ask around as well. With his help, we were made aware of a possible offer through a mutual friend. Needless to say, we were thrilled when we were able to purchase the former Rocconi property, on what was called

Middle Lake. Its location on a point, which jutted into the North Lake Channel, included 300 feet of waterfront and a small but wonderful cottage. Increasingly, this summer retreat became an important place for our family.

This was the site of many family work projects to improve the cottage and its environs. The building of a sturdy boat house, the construction of a rear porch and roof, the renovation of a spacious dock and the rip-rapping of the shoreline around the point are only some of the achievements that provided lessons for the kids in how working together brings the satisfaction of accomplishment. There was ample opportunity for play as well. A new boat provided the happy diversions of cruising and water skiing that we all enjoyed over many years. A campfire pit on the point was a friendly place to tell tall tales and gaze at the night-time stars.

The Spread Eagle cottage has also been the site of many gatherings with family and friends. Holidays, particularly the Fourth of July, have figured prominently in the almanac of Leonard family events. Birthdays, high school graduation parties and Leonard family reunions, such as the memorable one arranged for my mother's 80th birthday in the summer of 2002, were all pleasant affairs that took place at our family cottage.

The unmistakable scent of the needles shed from towering pines, the soft moist breeze drifting in off the lake, the glint of the sun reflected from the slowly rolling waters and the gentle lapping sound of the waves against the shore, all evoked an indelible memory of our Spread Eagle cottage, in the mind of each member of our family. It was our "Shangri-La"[57], our Heaven on earth and where each of us aspired to be, even when we were far from home. Someday, Kris and I will have our ashes cast from that sandy point and we will continue to live there in the memories of our children and grandchildren.

Such were the happy circumstances that existed for our young family as we faced into the optimistic decade of the 80's.

The Grandfathers; Clyde Randall and Ralph Leonard

Ray and Emma Leonard: March 31, 1945

"Buck" and Muriel Erickson: September 5, 1940

Emma and Ray and newborn son Stephen

The Leonard residence in Dearborn: 23737 Hollander

The Leonard cowboys: Steve, Mark and Clyde

Chuck and Kris Erickson

The Grosse Ile Leonard residence: 7954 Coventry

The Leonards: Clyde, Mark, Kim, Raymond, Emma, Ray and Steve

Steve and Kris: June 21, 1969

Muriel and granddaughter Erika

Steve and Kris

The Leonard Cottage at Spread Eagle in summer

Winter on the Spread Eagle Chain of Lakes

The Leonards: Gabe, Erika, Steve, Kris and Zach

Cottage work projects: Zach, Gabe and Steve

A younger Dr. Leonard

Cpl. Raymond Peter Weaver

Emma's 80th Birthday: Standing, L to R. John, Zach, Jim, Mark, Kris, Steve, Joyce, Ray, Sarah, Josh, Gabe, Susan, Clyde, Pete; Seated: Kim, Erika, Emma, Kara, Brenda, Luke and Raymond, Peter, Ian, Brock

Emma's children: Steve, Ray, Clyde, Mark and Kim

Emma's grandchildren: Luke, Zach, Josh, Gabe, Ian, Raymond, Kara, Peter, Brock and Erika

Jim and Erika Harbridge: August 30, 2003

Wedding Day: Emma, Steve, Kris, Erika, Jim, Zach, Claire, Gabe and Pete

The Brothers: Clyde, Steve and Mark

Pete, Lisa and Brock Weaver

Karen, Charles and Chuck: Lawrence University, 2003

Jeannie and Gabe: September 5, 2004

Jeannie and Gabe

Zach, Erika and Gabe Leonard

The Cousins: Kara, Josh and Luke

Zach and girlfriend Jill

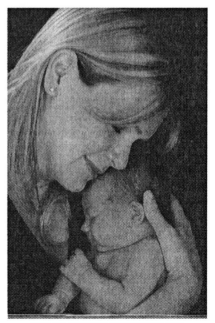
Erika and daughter Ava Kristine Harbridge

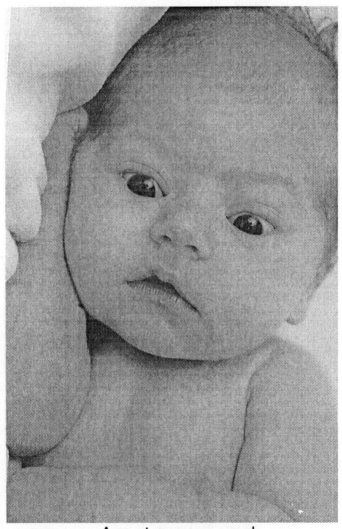

Ava at age one week

# CHAPTER 9

## LIFE AND DEATH IN THE FAMILY

The early years in Iron Mountain were a blur of family life and of building a medical practice. The constancy of the patient responsibility in a solo primary care type of practice was not daunting at first because I had been used to a fairly heavy load and time commitment during residency. Eventually it became clear, however, that unless I actually went out of town for a vacation or meeting that the phone would be ringing. It was less frequently my own patients calling and more frequently the hospital asking me to come see the latest emergency patient with medical complications from chronic illness or recent post-operative patients with medical complications. It became obvious that unless I had some coverage that I would not have time to see my kids grow or attend to the other non-medical things in life. This problem was remedied somewhat when two other doctors with internal medicine specialties started practice in town and we developed an association allowing for cross coverage of our patient care. That made a significant difference to me.

With some breathing room from medical practice I began to find time to pay more attention to my growing family, to read non-medical books and to teach myself some carpentry and construction skills, which came in handy at home and around our cottage. In addition, since I had always been interested in athletics, I joined a basketball team, sponsored by Dickinson

Homes, which played in the local men's league. Dickinson Homes was managed by Paul Santoni, a fellow player, who still is a friend. The competition and camaraderie we shared was gratifying. My association with that team lasted almost 20 years and with the friends and team-mates I met, even longer.

Living in an older home in town and owning an older cottage at the lake provided much raw material for my education in household maintenance skills. The considerable grounds surrounding these residences also supplied fodder for other landscaping and building projects. I had little skills in the manual trades before moving to Iron Mountain. However, I was eager to learn how to fix things and at the same time develop my knowledge and skill in woodworking, wiring, plumbing and landscaping. Little by little, I found that by consulting with those who knew such skills, I could steadily become proficient. I owe much to my brother-in-law Chuck who served as my mentor in this rudimentary period of my "manual arts" education. Completion of simple projects led to more complicated ones. Over time, this pursuit brought me immense satisfaction.

Rhythms exist in life that are basic to our nature and that can only be heard if we take a step back from the hurly-burly of everyday reality to listen for them. After years of frenetic, career related activity, a window of opportunity opened for me to find other melodies to which I could listen and learn, or in Kipling's exhortation to:

> Teach us delight in simple things,
> And mirth that has no bitter springs;[58]

In order to discover other parts of my nature, it was important for me to step back into these activities of reading, writing, working with my hands and participating in athletic competition. However, raising and guiding our kids was the greatest of these "delight(s) in simple things". Of the many aspects of raising children, one custom of particular importance to our young family took its germination then.

Kris began to realize the importance of eating together as a family. At first I resisted her attempt to do this since it was often hard to exactly determine when I would be home, especially if an emergency came up late in the day at the office or in the hospital. Kris saw the wisdom of this effort before me, however, and was insistent that we try to make it work as often as possible. With a little give and take, our family dinner time became a staple of our lives. Over time it became clear to us that this single habit contributed greatly to our shared feeling of being a strong family unit. Unfortunately, this is a custom ignored in too many families. The hectic pace and fast-food habits of our present society does not nurture our connection to the Judeo-Christian and Greco-Roman roots of the shared meal. There is indeed magic to the meal time[59]. This link to the ancient past can enrich us, if only we would establish it in our own homes.

The evening meal time gave our children the opportunity to discuss their daily activities. When they came to dinner from play or from school, they were free to vent about the frustrations or joys they may have had. The single ground rule was that nothing private or personal left the table. Kris, always the English teacher, tactfully corrected the kids in diction and encouraged them to present their ideas in coherent fashion. I used the dinner table to introduce interesting facts that I had recently read or learned. I challenged the kids, and often their friends, to think about these issues and answer questions that I posed. It was a time to enjoy the antics of the young and old. The "family dinner" became something which we all regarded with pleasant expectation. With Kris' considerable culinary skills, the food was abundant and delicious, but at our table there was more than that. In addition to the pleasing victuals, there was food for the soul. Even today, separated by distance as we all are, when we are able to visit and have those chances to gather for a "family dinner", we all look forward to this tradition with mutual anticipation.

Some things that happen in life make us think that the universe is governed by the laws of serendipity or that a Divine hand is moving events just to test our reaction and response. Something of that nature happened in 1983 when son Gabe, who was then in the first grade, went to the local roller rink to skate. About an hour prior to leaving the rink, an older boy, skating backwards, slammed into Gabe, pushing him onto the hard floor. Another older boy, who saw him crying, helped him up and washed the blood off his swollen lip. When Kris later picked him up and was startled by his injured face, Gabe did not dwell on how he was hurt, but rather on how he had been helped.

From her volunteer activities in the school, Kris was familiar with the "good Samaritan" who had helped her son. He was Raymond Peter Weaver, the son of Jack Weaver, who worked at the Michigan Employment Office in Iron Mountain. Jack was a single father raising Peter and his older sisters. Their mother had left the family and was no longer in the area. Suspecting that he would like to hear about his son's good deed, Kris called Jack and complimented him on his fine son. Then, because Gabe asked if his "hero" could baby-sit for us, it was not long before "Pete" was around our house frequently; babysitting, interacting and helping out. Kris became a substitute mother for Pete and over time he became one of the family to us all.

Pete was older than our three kids and his experiences throughout his high school years were somewhat of a practice run for Kris and me. Since he had missed some basic skills in the elementary grades with his family's separation, Pete struggled as a student. However, he was a good athlete and excelled in basketball, baseball, soccer and football. He was an example of a youngster who used athletics as the bond that kept his head in school and kept him working toward a goal.

Our family enjoyed following Pete's athletic career. By his senior year of high school, the basketball coach at Lakeland College recruited Pete to be the point guard on his college team. After a year of successful play, Pete surprised all of us, and particularly his dad Jack. He realized that college was not right for him at that time and decided to join the Marines. Within a short time, he left in a tearful goodbye for basic training at Camp

Pendleton. That was the summer of 1989. After successful completion of basic training and a graduation ceremony that his proud father Jack was able to attend, he transferred to 29 Palms for desert training. This coincided with the onset of the Gulf War, so desert training was a military priority.

Pete's subsequent involvement in Desert Shield and Desert Storm was a worrisome time for all of us. Kris, with motherly concern, was on a first name basis with the Marine Information Officer, whom she called frequently to get any news of Pete and his Light Armored Vehicle (LAV) unit. His plain-spoken but articulate letters home from their desert assignment were read with vigilant silence by each of us.

U.S. forces won a decisive victory in Iraq and Kuwait and, fortunately, Pete stayed out of harm's way. He was then deployed with his unit to Somalia for a short period of time. Luckily for him, however, the marines were moved out of Somalia and the army deployed in their place before a fateful incident occurred, involving the attack on the Army's Blackhawk Helicopters in 1992, an incident which has been the subject of a book and a movie more recently[60]. I take no joy in the fact that the marines were spared from this fight, but it is clear in retrospect that those poor army units were not supported as they should have been and that the decision was made at the highest level. That being the case, I was happy that Pete was no longer in Somalia. Another deployment followed to Okinawa, and after a total of four years in the corps, Pete was honorably discharged. We were all proud of Pete's service to our country. Our course together with him was one of serendipity. It is impossible to speculate on how different our experience would have been if Gabe had not gone skating that night in 1983.

It was during these interesting years that my relationship with my brother-in-law Chuck became more personal and close. While our initial reactions to each other were like mixing oil and water, that was only superficial and evolved. A pivotal point in our relationship occurred when Chuck and Karen's only son, Charles Martin Erickson, adopted in 1979, had a nearly disastrous illness in his second year of life. He developed a severe case of bacterial meningitis, which I was able to diagnose in its early stage. It was then necessary to arrange with a pediatrician to transfer him to Green Bay, where he was successfully treated. From that time on, Chuck and I felt a new closeness, not only as relatives, but also as friends.

Subsequently, young "Chuck" became an exemplary student as he progressed in school. He developed an interest and talent in music, both voice and instrumental. Graduating from Iron Mountain in the top of his class in 1997, he enrolled at Lawrence University in Appleton, Wisconsin. There he graduated with honors in 2003, having a double major in Music and Spanish. Kris and I attended Chuck's senior voice recital in the spring of 2002 and were impressed at his masterful abilities. Charles M. Erickson, Jr. is now working toward a Masters Degree in College Administration at Iowa State University and will take a position with that university as a college administrator upon completion of that program.

With regard to the Senior Chuck Erickson, his position as the superintendent of equipment at Bacco Road Construction was very demanding. He, in turn, was a very demanding boss of his crews of mechanics and laborers. Remarkably, he is one of those individuals who had all his life had a singular love for what he eventually did for a living. Since he was very young, he loved heavy equipment and mechanical things, so he was a natural as an equipment superintendent. Even in his spare time he was involved with similar pursuits. To that end, he constructed a large metal shop building at the Erickson/Johnson family camp in Norway, Michigan. It rivaled any such building in the commercial world. He did all of this so he could continue to fix and maintain his considerable collection of "toys". Chuck was the personification of the adage that "the guy who dies with the most toys, wins".

His skills in the trades extended to construction of all types; electrical, plumbing, woodworking and metal fabrication. He was a treasure trove of information for me in my burgeoning amateur career in these areas. He was always available to help me with complications in my own projects and to this day I still enjoy working with him on his own projects. Using Chuck's unique assortment of equipment, we constructed a sturdy boat house and dock system at my cottage, in addition to other remarkable projects. Although we constantly quibble with each other as we work, a habit that drives others crazy, we enjoy each other immensely.

There was another side of Chuck that was as serious and deeply ingrained as his love of mechanical things. That was his love for history, and in particular, his love for the history of World War II. Without a doubt, Chuck was one of the most knowledgeable people I had ever known on this subject. With his singular zeal for researching the war, he had collected an exemplary film and reading library on the subject. With his own unique perspective of mechanical equipment, he knew the war not just from a political or military standpoint, but literally from the nuts and bolts of battle, the "sinews" of the war. He talked of the trucks, guns, tanks, planes and other details in a way that no other "usual" military historian could.

My experiences with Chuck have taught me that people who lacked formal (i.e.-college) education could nevertheless have considerable knowledge of subjects usually considered "academic". I have noted this in other similarly educated individuals and in a variety of ways. These people, because of their practical approach to life, were often more intelligent and knowledgeable in a common sense, worldly sort of way than many of those learned spokesmen from government and academia. Impressive credentials do not always command respect; what matters most is clear-headed analysis not clouded by preconception and always based on an awareness of human nature. Chuck's interest in history was a real stimulus to me in those years. Increasingly, I began to share this interest with him. I found myself drawn to similar study and discovery. Over time, the study of history in all its forms has become a priority for me. Chuck and I continue to enjoy discussing many aspects of human history and can see mutual parallels to events occurring in the present day. All of this was a happy denouement to what started out as mere "oil and water".

During that same period of time, new developments were unfolding in the extended Leonard family. Clyde and Susan both pursued careers in education after graduation from Indiana University. Clyde eventually became a school administrator and Susan taught special education. In 1985 Clyde became the high school principal in South Knox, Indiana, where he lived for nine years. With a subsequent offer of work in a larger school district, he then moved with his family to Mt. Carmel, Illinois, in 1994, where he is still the principal of the Mt. Carmel High School and where Susan is still teaching in the same system. They are family-oriented, religious individuals and their successful efforts in raising children are a credit to them and to everyone in our family.

Clyde and Susan's three children were born at approximately the same times as our own children. Their first child, Joshua Clyde Leonard, was born on October 19, 1974. A tall and intelligent young man, he became his high school senior class valedictorian and attended college at Evansville University for premedical training. Josh graduated with honors from Southern Illinois University Medical School in 2001, followed by a (current) cardiology fellowship at Wake Forest University Medical School. He was married to the former Sara Shasteen. Their first child, Samuel Joshua Leonard, born on March 25, 2004, was the first of the next generation of Leonard's.

Lucas Randall Leonard, Clyde and Susan's second son, was born on July 20, 1976. Luke grew to be a serious-minded, patriotic young man who won an appointment to West Point, where he distinguished himself over four years and graduated in 1999. Like his brother, Luke decided to follow a medical career and attended medical school at the University of Illinois-College of Medicine at Rockford. He was chosen by his classmates to give the graduation address in 2003 and made all of us proud with his stirring words. Luke married the former Brenda Haberman. Currently, they are both in Honolulu where Capt. Lucas Leonard is taking his Medical Residency at the Tripler Army Medical Center. I was pleased to learn that Josh and his brother Luke both considered medical careers, in part, because of my influence. I was honored to be considered in this light, to be sure.

Kara Susan Leonard was born March 13, 1979, the last of the Clyde and Susan Leonard brood. Kara grew to be a pretty, young woman who graduated in education from Evansville University in 2001. She taught middle school math in Atlanta for three years, then successfully competed for a consultant position with Thomson Publishing Company, a secondary school textbook publisher. Kara's smile lights up the room she is in. She is a fun-loving member of the family who enjoys singing and dancing, an ability she comes by honestly in the Leonard tradition.

Many times, Clyde and I have remarked that our kids, being close in age and in interests, have fed off of each others' accomplishments. It was as if the knowledge that one cousin's success motivated the other to perform equally as well. They have not only been successful at each stage of life thus far, but they are good-hearted, interesting people and enjoy being together when the occasion permits. Assuredly, they are all worthy emissaries of the Leonard family name.

My brother Mark has been known as "Uncle Mark", not only to all his nieces and nephews, but to their friends as well. He was always a natural entertainer who has provided much sidesplitting laughter for the Leonard family over the years. Mark was a talented high school athlete, excelling in football, basketball, and track. He was especially accomplished in the high jump and competed at the collegiate level. He was perhaps the most talented athlete in the Ray and Emma Leonard family. In 1979, Mark purchased property on Belleville Lake near Detroit and had a dream that one day he would have a great home on that site. While working at Ford Motor Company, he used their schooling plan to return to the college courses that he left behind at Ashland College in the late 1960's. He completed his education with distinction, graduating with a B.S.N. from Henry Ford Community College in

1987. Mark continued to work toward his dream home while working two jobs, one at Ford and one in nursing. He saw his dream come true when his home was built in 1991. Retiring from Ford Motor Company on New Year's Day, 2004, he continues to work in nursing and to enhance his property. But above all, Mark has been a beloved uncle to all his nieces and nephews and over the years has faithfully cheered them on in all their endeavors.

My sister Kim also stopped her college career early to work. She then met and married John Chickering Simpson on September 18, 1982. John, a true Southern Indiana boy, enjoys fine dining, concerts, cars, motorcycles and especially travel. He has been a very savvy and successful investor in real estate in the college town of Bloomington, Indiana. Between a sales position for various intra-ocular lens companies and his own rental real estate holdings, John has been a successful businessman. He and Kimmy built a beautiful home on a high oak ridge outside Bloomington. A winding road weaves through a stand of pines to where the house suddenly opens into view. Amish builders constructed this unusual home, which features a large great room with beautiful maple floors, a spacious kitchen, a large art studio, and a multilevel deck off the back. The cabinets as well as much of the furniture there are hand-crafted out of beautiful woods. The home is also decorated with many of my sister's paintings. Always a good painter, Kim decided to return to school to earn her degree in Fine Arts from Indiana University, graduating with honors in 1996. Since that time, her paintings have been shown in various local studios in Bloomington and Indianapolis and are in great demand. She and John travel abroad frequently and are always looking for the next interesting place to visit.

My youngest brother Raymond, who attended high school in Stockton, California, was also a good athlete. His game was tennis and he played it well enough to play for Indiana University, ably competitive at the Division I level of play. Graduating from I.U. with a degree in business, he took a position with Cook Group Incorporated, a Bloomington company that makes radiological and cardiac catheters and other medical devices. (This was the same company that would employ my daughter Erika in the mid 1990's.) Raymond married Joyce Alvarez on September 12, 1987, in Valparaiso, Indiana. Although Raymond's job took them to various places including Chicago and the San Francisco area, they eventually settled in Bloomington where they are raising their three boys. Their first son, Ian Leonard, was born on February 11, 1991, while Ray and Joyce lived in Tracy, California. Raymond Leonard III was born in Bloomington on March 8, 1993, and then Peter Leonard was born there on August 28, 1995. These youngsters are growing up in the town of my birth and where their paternal grandparents returned to live. Their progress in school and sports is remarkable. If early indications are correct, they will make their mark in life in admirable fashion.

Death and loss are as much a part of life as happiness and gain. Death came to our family in these years as it comes to all families of humankind. The first loss to the family was the death of Kris' father, "Buck" Erickson. In the early 1970's Buck developed cancer of the throat which was assuredly related to years of smoking. Like my own father and many others of the World War II generation, cigarettes were the ubiquitous salve for trouble and angst. Buck was an inveterate smoker from his days as a Staff Sgt. in the U.S. Army, where he served in the military police during the Detroit riots of 1942 and later as an Army News Correspondent. He continued to smoke heavily during his newspaper days, and the toll caught up with him in the 70's. The diagnosis of his disease was made in Iron Mountain and resulted in a major disfiguring surgery at Woods V.A. Hospital in Milwaukee. In spite of his successful recovery from that surgery, he remained in poor health. After a relatively short period of time, Buck died in his sleep in 1974, at the young age of 57.

A decade and a half later, in the spring of 1989, Kris' mother Muriel suddenly had a stroke while working in her yard. Muriel was a stabilizing force in her family for years. As previously mentioned, when we moved back to Iron Mountain in 1976 she was instrumental in getting the business end of my practice up and running. Prior to our move, she decided to retire from her work at the hospital, wanting to spend as much time with her growing grandchildren as she could. Our children have especially fond memories of their grandmother Muriel, who always predictably spoiled them as only grandmothers could. When the stroke occurred I determined that it was likely due to a leaking aneurysm and immediately transferred her to Green Bay. There, she underwent neurosurgery to repair the leak and a difficult, prolonged rehabilitation period. However, with the passage of time, the hope for her return to normal dimmed. Paralyzed on one side, unable to speak, to walk independently or to take care of herself, Muriel spent almost three years in a local nursing home before contracting pneumonia and dying in her 75th year in May of 1992. These were three difficult years for Kris who made daily visits to Muriel and who had to contend with her mother languishing in a state of utter dependence. Death, when it came, was a blessing. Although she was to be sorely missed, everyone knew that this vibrant lady suffered greatly in her condition as it was.

The loss of my father Ray Leonard in the late 1980's was also a significant blow to our whole family. Still short of retirement, he and Mom moved back to Bloomington, Indiana to live, where he traveled around the state as a fund raiser for the Indiana Foundation. They had been up to Iron Mountain in the fall of 1988 for a visit, where amazingly, Dad learned to water ski for the first time. His sons were with him there at Spread Eagle and he was so proud of his accomplishment; we were equally so of him.

However, later in the fall, after his return home, he began to have back pains that were more than the usual muscular strain. After a visit to a doctor in Bloomington he was diagnosed as having cancer in the spine, probably from a primary source in the lung, most likely related to the years of cigarette smoking, as earlier noted. Because of the diffuse nature of the problem at diagnosis, his cancer was not amenable to curative treatment, but rather to palliation. His condition quickly deteriorated and Dad died at the hospital in Bloomington on March 27, 1987.

Following the funeral, the family procession took Dad's casket 120 miles through a spring snowstorm to Aurora, Indiana for burial. He was laid to rest at the Riverview Cemetery, where the gravesites date back to before the Revolutionary War. An official brass plaque, now on his own gravesite, details the military service during WWII of this patriot and our beloved father. The death of Raymond B. Leonard was only four days short of his 42$^{nd}$ wedding anniversary. He was 63 years of age. With his death, the proud patriarch of the Leonard family passed the torch to the next generation, and with God's Grace, we will carry it onward.

# CHAPTER 10

## THE DECADE OF OPTIMISM

In spite of the deaths that occurred in our family, there remained a distinct sense of optimism among us throughout the 1980's and into the 1990's. Optimism is a Leonard characteristic and my father, in particular, exemplified this trait during his lifetime. Of the many blessings in our lives from which optimism could spring, foremost was the health and growth of our children. At the end of the decade of the 1980's, Erika was already in high school and Gabe and Zach soon followed. My medical practice was well established, and it was reassuring that Kris was able to devote her time to the upbringing of our kids. These personal and family related matters were also impacted by the new sense of confidence in the nation at large, resulting in large part from the Reagan legacy. An examination of the background of that legacy is in order.

Optimism is an American characteristic that is as old as the hopeful explorers and settlers that came to our shores. America was to be, in John Winthrop's words, "a shining city on a hill". This man, the first governor of the Massachusetts Bay colony in the mid 1600's, viewed the new land as part of a religious covenant. The notion of a divinely chosen country and its people was an invocation of the Biblical verses of a "new Jerusalem" of Revelations 21:1 and "A city that is set on an hill cannot be hid" of Matthew 5:14. The idea of "American exceptionalism" is only a modern day term for the feeling that our founders had about the land and people they knew in the new world. It is however, the cornerstone of the debate between the present day multiculturalists and conservatives. In his Farewell Address to the Nation in January, 1989, Ronald Reagan also used the metaphor of a "city on a hill". He eloquently said, "In my mind it was a tall proud city built on rocks stronger than oceans, wind-swept, God-blessed, and teeming with people of all kinds living in harmony and peace, a city with free ports that hummed with commerce and creativity, and if there had to be city walls, the walls had doors and the doors were open to anyone with the will and the heart to get there". This lengthy image conjured the inclusive vision of optimism that characterized the man who was called the "great communicator"[61].

George Washington, the "Father of our Country", also expressed optimism about the American experiment. In his Farewell Address of September, 1796, he said, "Profoundly penetrated with this idea, I carry it with me to my grave, as a strong incitement to unceasing vows that Heaven may continue to you the choicest tokens of its beneficence; that your union and brotherly affection may be perpetual; that the free constitution, which is the work of your hands, may be sacredly maintained; that its administration in every department may be stamped with wisdom and may be made complete, by so careful a preservation and so prudent a use of this blessing as acquire to them the glory of recommending it to the applause, the affection; and adoption of every nation which is yet a stranger to it"[62].

Adding that divine guidance would be needed he cautioned, "Religion and morality are indispensable supports . . . And let us with caution indulge the supposition, that morality can be maintained without religion. Whatever may be conceded to the influence of refined education on minds peculiar structure; reason and experience both forbid us to expect that national morality can prevail in exclusion of religious principle". These statements, from two of our greatest national leaders, suggested that their optimism for our country arose from their faith that if America does not forsake the Almighty then the Almighty will look favorably on her.

Sometimes, astute judgment about American character has emanated from those not native to this land. For example, Alexis De Tocqueville, the famous French statesman and author, traveled extensively around this land in the decade of the 1830's. He published many diaries and most significantly, a multi-volume book entitled *Democracy in America*. His recollections and comments on many aspects of American culture and character were insightful then and even continue to be expressly so today. He wrote of hardworking, individualistic, and religious Americans who had an innate, optimistic view of the life they would forge in this new world. His comments in the chapter "Of the Taste for Physical Well-Being in America" were particularly instructive. "I never met in America with any citizen so poor as not to cast a glance of hope and envy on the enjoyments of the rich, or whose imagination did not possess itself by anticipation of those good things which fate still obstinately withheld from him. On the other hand, I never perceived amongst the wealthier inhabitants of the United States that proud contempt of physical gratifications which is sometimes to be met with even in the most opulent and dissolute aristocracies. Most of these wealthy persons were once poor; they have felt the sting of want; they were long a prey to adverse fortunes; and now that the victory is won, the passions which accompanied the contest have survived it; their minds are, as it were, intoxicated by the small enjoyment which they have pursued for forty years".

In De Toqueville's preceding chapter, "That the Americans Apply the Principle of Interest Rightly Understood to Religious Matters", he detailed that the American search for prosperity in this world was balanced by religious belief in the next. Americans were optimistic about their ability to achieve comfort in the material sense, but it came in conjunction with religious perspective. It is part of Ancient Judeo-Christian thought that "Man doth not live by bread only" as recorded in the Pentateuch (Deuteronomy 8:3). De Tocqueville thus recorded the religious nature of the citizenry and in his overall view confirmed that the optimism of Americans was widespread and abiding[63].

Having conjectured that optimism was an American characteristic and that it diffused from the leaders of our land to individual citizens, how did this factor apply to the decade of the 1980's and beyond and how did it relate to the previously mentioned "Reagan legacy?" To begin with, Ronald Reagan did many remarkable and lasting things for the nation. He restored a sense of pride in our country by building up the military and using the bully pulpit to give a positive and uplifting message to his countrymen. He lowered taxes from a confiscatory 70% level to 28% and turned around the floundering economy using supply side economics. However, his greatest achievement and the cause for the preponderance of optimism in the majority of us was the defeat of communism, culminating in the end of the four-decade long Cold War.

Perhaps the fact that the Cold War ran for so long and encompassed so many changes in leadership may have something to do with why the Cold War has not had the attention it deserves. World War I and World War II were better defined in the public memory than the nebulous period of the Cold War. In fact, this war actually encompassed the Korean War and the Vietnam War if we consider these wars to have sprung from the policy of containment of communism in its Soviet or Red Chinese variants. Memorials in Washington, D.C. for over 100,000 GI's from those conflicts attest to the fact that the Cold War could get very hot and that it was always deadly serious. It was also deadly serious for many patriotic Americans who fought the clandestine war of CIA and Special Forces engagements over those forty years and who often cannot be properly acknowledged for their service because the details are still classified.

Winston Churchill, who may be the greatest republican statesman in history, recognized the repressive character of Soviet Communism early on. Even when England was forced to go into partnership with the Russian bear out of necessity to defeat Nazism, Churchill never doubted who his erstwhile ally Stalin was or what his intentions were. As the Second World War progressed and Great Britain took somewhat of a back seat to the might of the Americans and the Russians, Churchill tried unsuccessfully to convince Roosevelt that Russian intentions should be stymied by joint British and American planning.

He especially attempted to engineer advance coordination at the Yalta Conference in January, 1945, but was rebuffed by FDR[64]. The reasons for this are not entirely clear and perhaps Roosevelt's poor health blurred his vision of the Soviet intent; after all, he died on April 12th of the same year. However, it is sadly true that Roosevelt had much earlier in the war indicated a naiveté about Stalin that was disconcerting. He had written Churchill in March, 1942, "I know you will not mind my being brutally frank when I tell you that I think that I can personally handle Stalin better than either your Foreign Office or my State Department, Stalin hates the guts of all your top people. He thinks he likes me better, and I hope he will continue to do so"[65]. In the aftermath of the Yalta accords, Stalin showed his true nature by breaking his word on all the conditions, resulting in the Soviet domination of Eastern Europe and much of the Balkans. This was in essence the real start of the Cold War.

Churchill gave this new war further emphasis in Fulton, Missouri on March 5, 1946, when he gave his "Sinews of Peace Address"[66]. He described the growing Soviet menace and spoke of the need for England and America to nurture "the special relationship" that they had developed over their joint history to resist the expansionist threat. "From Stettin in the Baltic to Trieste in the Adriatic, an iron curtain has descended across the continent. Behind that line lie all the capitals of the ancient states of Central and Eastern Europe. Warsaw, Berlin, Prague, Vienna, Budapest, Belgrade, Bucharest and Sofia, all these famous cities and the populations around them lie in what I must call the Soviet sphere, and all are subject in one form or another, not only to Soviet influence but to a very high and, in many cases, increasing measure of control from Moscow."

The "Iron Curtain" speech, as it became known in the popular press set the stakes for the West in the Cold War Years. Harry

Truman quickly became cognizant of how to deal with Soviet duplicity after Roosevelt's death. At home he formed what would become the CIA and purged his administration of any pro-Soviet elements, which resulted in the sacking of Henry Wallace, his Secretary of Agriculture. Abroad, Truman announced the "Truman Doctrine" which averred "that it must be the policy of the United States to support free peoples who are resisting attempted subjugation by armed minorities or outside pressure". He unveiled the Marshall Plan which started in 1948 and spent $10.2 billion over the next three years to rebuild war-torn Western Europe. When Stalin blocked access to Western Berlin in 1948, the Berlin airlift began with up to 8,000 tons a day flown in until the Russians stood down in May, 1949. "Give 'em Hell Harry" was a formidable foe of the Soviet and Chinese threat but it was on his watch that America became embroiled in the Korean War. It took Eisenhower to disengage us from that bloody conflict.

Dwight David Eisenhower was certainly one of America's most under-rated Presidents. After his election to the presidency in 1952, he cultivated a public persona of a kindly, but disengaged, former military man who liked to play golf, ostensibly while smart guys like Sherman Adams, his chief of staff, and John Foster Dulles, his Secretary of State, did the heavy lifting[67]. Paul Johnson, the British historian, and others, termed Eisenhower's style of governing as "pseudo-delegation"[68]. Even Adams and Dulles were under the impression that they were in charge of the domestic and international situations respectively. They had no real idea that every morning Eisenhower contacted his domestic and foreign out posts and made the crucial decisions from behind the public scene. The release of Ike's phone records and personal transcripts in the 1970's documented a man very much in charge and a true "cold warrior". If it were it not for his firm attention to the global containment of the communist threat, it was doubtful that the course of the Cold War would have had the same outcome.

In 1960, President Kennedy became the new commander-in-chief of the cold war effort. His administration began with the strong statements of his Inaugural Address. In October, 1962 however, the confrontation with Khrushchev over the Cuban missile crisis came very close to tactical nuclear exchange. His Secretary of Defense, Robert McNamara coined the MAD hypothesis of "mutually assured destruction" in relation to the nuclear arsenals of the major powers. The final resolution of the crisis has garnered mixed reviews. The Russians backed down in Cuba, but the tradeoff included a decrement of our missiles in Turkey, a fact less well known. In similar style, Kennedy also advanced the theory of the "Domino Effect", which contended that one communist victory in Asia would result in all the other countries in that region converting to communism. The Vietnam War and its domestic controversy overshadowed much of JFK's role in the further resolution of the Cold War, just as it did during the administrations of Johnson and Nixon. However, Nixon's attempt to normalize relations with China in the early 1970's was one effort that may have further strained the Sino-Soviet rift, putting additional pressure on the failing Soviet system, even at a time when its global deployments seemed robust.

During the subsequent period of the superpower contest, the post Vietnam years, the Watergate years and the Carter years represent times of weakness in the West's ability to respond to the challenge of the Cold War. In its anemic state, the American policy of containment became the policy of détente, as if we were unable to directly respond to the communist juggernaut. Cowed by the knowledge of multiple missiles pointed at them, the populace lived in a state of fearful insecurity. Throughout the period of the 1950's and through the 1970's children were taught about such things as bomb shelters and nuclear winter in our schools. High gas prices and rising interest rates in the latter part of these years deepened the public depression. It took a new paradigm from a new president to change this stalemate.

It was reported that in 1977, while still Governor of California, Ronald Reagan asked Richard Allen if he would like to hear his theory of the Cold War[69]. Mr. Allen would become Reagan's first national security advisor in 1980, during his first presidency. "Some people think I'm simplistic", said Reagan, "but there's a difference between being simplistic and being simple. My theory of the Cold War is that we win and they lose."

Allen replied, "Governor, do you mean that?"

"Mr. Reagan replied", 'Of course I mean it. I just said it!'

Allen later said, "I was flabbergasted; I'd worked for Nixon and Goldwater and many others, and I'd heard a lot about . . . détente and the need to manage the Cold War, but never did I hear a leading politician put the goal so starkly".

This interchange encapsulates the out-of-the-box thinking that was required for America to quit "managing" and instead start "winning" the Cold War. This incisive statement was what a man of life-long reading and thinking about basic principles would say. It resulted from a clear headed analysis of the evil nature of communism, a system whose thick boots squashed the aspirations of men who were meant to be free. His insightful knowledge of communism's internal inconsistencies revealed that the contradictions of that system could be exploited to produce its own defeat[70]. Reagan's vision arose from a deep faith in God and a belief in the essential goodness, strength and the resiliency of the American system. This was definitely not the kind of viewpoint that would be expected from one of the intelligentsia whether from the political, press or academic variants. These commentators found the mere "simplicity" of such thinking to be anathema and deplored any who deigned to do so.

The same people who considered Reagan a reckless cowboy in his statements and actions were the same people who pandered to Soviet Communism and excused or minimized the ills of that regime. The "useful idiots" have survived beyond the Cold War and can still be found writing the apologias for the remnants of communism today. The totalitarian regimes of Cuba, Red China, North Korea and Vietnam still have their voices here in this country. By and large, these were the same people who denied that Reagan really defeated communism. They asserted that Communism was going to fail anyway; Reagan was just lucky enough to be around when it did. However, Reagan understood that any country in which it took ten years for a citizen to buy a car was not capable of competing with regard to a military buildup and the construction of SDI. These intellectual folks did not understand that simple paradox and thus, did not anticipate the incipient downfall.

Perhaps it is overt malicious intent to deny the recognition that Reagan deserves in this matter. Perhaps some genuinely believe that the question actually revolves around the old saw of whether historical forces or great individuals determine history. Some thought that Russian Communism was capable of "reform", but Reagan knew that was leftist delusion. Mikhail Gorbachev, that idol of the left, attempted reform with no result. If that "impossible dream" of the left was successful, who knows how long the Soviets might have lasted. Nonetheless, one thing is certain. Soviet Communism fell and it happened when Ronald Reagan was president. When asked during the Reagan Funeral, who won the Cold War; Lady Margaret Thatcher was emphatic, Ronald Reagan did[71]. When all is said and done, the controversy becomes moot when we remember the statement on a plaque that Reagan kept in the Oval Office during his presidency. To paraphrase, it is surprising how much can be accomplished when no one cares who gets the credit. I can only imagine that the "Gipper" is smiling at us from the grave on this one.

Without a doubt, the end of the Cold War was an event commensurate with the end of other great wars. When considering the magnitude of lives lost in the long bloody chapter of Soviet Communism, Stalin's purges and engineered famines may have sent several tens of millions to a premature graves and with untold suffering. Alexander Solzhenitsyn gave us the horrific details of the Gulag where so many nameless individuals perished. In his *Black Book of Communism*, Nicolas Werth, a co-author, told of the Russian Red Terror which emphasized the elimination of whole classes of people. He compared the "class genocide" of communism with the "race genocide" of Nazism and pointed out that, although both were "crimes against humanity", the magnitude of the communists far outdistanced the Holocaust[72]. This is not a comfortable comparison for left-leaning ideologues, who have always vigorously condemned fascism but have embraced that proposed brand of human perfectibility known as communism. In point of fact, these are only two sides of the same coin.

The Soviets fought valiantly against the Nazi's and lost greatly in the Second World War. Although the bravery of Russian troops is unquestionable, they often fought with inadequate supplies and under the pressure that they would be shot by their own troops if they did not engage the enemy. The Russians probably lost 20 million people in the WW II war effort, but ironically, at the time of their sacrifice, Stalin had the prisons full of their own countrymen. Again to quote Werth, "the Soviet prisons had never held as many prisoners as they did in the year of victory: a grand total of nearly 5.5 million people".

In a related fashion, the Red Chinese brand of communism is not a kinder, gentler form of the same governing regime. Under Mao similar mass famines were engineered, similar purges of classes of citizens took place. On June 4, 1989, Chinese students, who had erected a 30 foot fiber-and-glass replica of the Statue of Liberty, paid dearly when Red Army troops opened fire on them and other bystanders using tanks and infantry. Twenty-six hundred people were killed and over ten thousand injured. The massacre of Tiananmen Square[73] demonstrated, once again the brutal nature of communism, here in its Chinese form. This is the same regime that, with a few changes, is now being "engaged" by Western democracies in an attempt to bring about improvement without conflict through trade and commerce. It is also the regime whose nuclear program was abetted by Clinton-era computer upgrades given under questionable circumstances[74]. Thus, while the Soviet missile silos were taken down, we now can contemplate that Chinese missiles, with improved guidance systems, are armed and pointed at the United States. This Chinese example of communism poses a real question mark for the future and a problem for all our future leaders.

In spite of all of these caveats, the overall picture was bright as the 1980's came to a close. On Reagan's trip to the Brandenburg

Gate of the Berlin Wall on June 12, 1987, he said, "Mr. Gorbachev, open this gate! Mr. Gorbachev, tear down this wall!" After devastating losses in Afghanistan, Soviet troops pulled out in early 1989. Deep unilateral cuts in Soviet armed forces in Western Europe ensued. Elections were forced by democratic forces in Poland and Lech Walesa, the head of the Solidarity Party, was elected president. Eric Honaker, the East German dictator, was toppled and on the night of November 9, 1989 crowds of East Germans took hammers and picks to the Berlin Wall and pulled it down[75]. Thereafter, events moved quickly both within and from without the Soviet Empire, resulting in new governments that displaced the old. What began with *Glasnost* and *Perestroika* under Gorbachev inexorably led to the dissolution of the Soviet state. Communism could not be reformed, it could only be replaced. By 1991 the dissolution was complete. Millions who, in the future might have been subjected to the weight of Soviet communism, had considerable reason to be grateful. For the millions who had already perished under it, many nameless and without a trace, there were no further earthly rewards available.

It was of interest that as the World War II Memorial opened in Washington, D.C. on Memorial Day 2004, another group had been planning a "Victims of Communism Memorial" in the same city[76]. Lee Edwards, the acting director of the Foundation for that memorial had been seeking approval from the National Capital Memorial Commission. Efforts are currently underway to complete the approval and funding process, with the expectation that this memorial will be under construction by the summer of 2005. This would be a fitting tribute to not only the 100 million who lost their lives in the Cold War but also to the succession of leaders whose efforts brought this sorry chapter of history to a close.

As the 1990's came into view there was indeed much cause for optimism, both in the Leonard family and the world around it.

# CHAPTER 11

## MOVING THROUGH THE YEARS OF SCHOOLING

Although Pete's high school years gave us some impression of what was to come from kids in their high school years, it was not a complete preparation for dealing with Erika's sojourn into that challenging land. Anyone who has had both boys and girls of adolescent age will attest that the vicissitudes of the male offspring are nothing compared to that of the female. It is an understatement to say that teenage girls are more of a test to parental skill than boys by some yet to be determined mathematical factor. This is not to say that the raising of daughters is not just as satisfying or perhaps more so than boys, it is just more complicated. The highs and lows are of greater magnitude and the duration of the lows is often complicated by the jealousies of the female peer group.

Boys tend to fight out their differences in brief but physical confrontations. They then put those differences behind them. Girls use much more subtle and emotional tactics when they are at odds and can be positively mean and hurtful to each other. The aftermath persists longer and is more difficult to repair. Erika experienced some of these peer group altercations and although they made her young life difficult along the way, her basic sunny disposition was never changed.

When Erika was young she displayed an acute sensitivity to the loss and grief that life can bring that was beyond her years.

Perceptively, she wrote a poignant tribute to her life-long friend and companion Keisha, our faithful dog. Since the early days in Detroit, this dog had been her protector and side-kick. By the early 1980's, when Erika was in the 5th grade, Keisha's general health had deteriorated and she was especially hobbled with painful arthritis. We all knew that the humane course was for her to be "put down". I discussed the problem with Erika, wanting her to know my plan to take our dog to the vet to be put to sleep. She left for school one day knowing that she would not see her dog again. This proved to be an example of how children "know" something but do not realize the full impact of it. When Erika returned from school to find me burying Keisha in the woods by our house, she was grief-stricken. It was the first time that she experienced the cold reality of loss in her life. Her subsequent written encomium was and is still a memorable composition for a young girl of that age. Her teacher found it exceptional and submitted it for publication in the school's creative writing booklet. I include it here in its entirety.

## Keisha

Keisha was my dog. I had her since I was born. She was great! When we lived in Detroit I could not of played out side if we did not have Keisha. She baby sat me when I was playing. She was playmate and best friend. When we moved to Iron Mountain I did not need someone to watch me outside. Then when I started to go to school and stuff. I started to forget about her. The time came when she was old and suffering and my mom and dad said pretty soon we would have to put her to sleep. I did not think about it cause I was late for school. It was really sad watching her suffer she had bad arthritis, she could not get in the car and she was very slow. Pretty soon we put her to sleep. I did not worry about it but then when I got home my dad was burying her in the back yard. Chrissy was with me. I went back there. I saw my dad crying. He hugged me and I started to cry too. Keisha was like a first child to my mom and dad and to me she was like a sister. I did not know how much I loved her intell she was gone. The next day I cried all day. I was so mad I was going to go out and dig her up. But as I was going my mom caught me. I missed her so much and it had only been a day she was dead. Chrissy came over and we went to her grave. We both started to cry hard. The only thing I could think of was her and her sad eyes she would give me when I said no and how they made me say yes. Keisha was my best friend in the whole word. And she still is. I wish she was still alive. She was the greatest dog a person could ever want.

The End

Erika Leonard

Erika always had a fun-loving, bright disposition and her delightful laugh was infectious. Her brothers always counted on her to respond to their antics with that sunny, mirthful laughter that would light up the household even when their jokes were not particularly funny. Our dinner table usually resonated with her laughter. In high school, Erika was involved in many fun-loving activities, some related to school and others extra-curricular in nature. She was an excellent student academically, graduating in the upper 10% of her class. She was involved in cheerleading and tennis for four years, in spite of the limitations that asthma placed on her. In her freshman year she won the Third Singles Championship of the Mid-Peninsula Conference in Girl's Tennis. Asthma was always a factor and she sometimes had to forfeit tennis matches midway through due to her difficulty in breathing.

Her high school years were full of school and social activities, racing from one thing to another at break neck-speed, always just short of being late for the next event. On school mornings for example, her brothers waited impatiently for her to get ready so they could all get to school without tardy detentions. At the last minute she would fly down the stairs, still attending to details of fixing her clothing and hair. Only later did we find out that, in fact, on most mornings her brother Gabe drove her car to school while Erika continued to put on make-up or comb her hair. During those years, her brother was only 13 or 14 and, of course, did not have a driver's license!

After graduation from high school Erika enrolled at Michigan State University. She took her prerequisite courses in the first years and applied to their nursing school. This was our first personal brush with the realities of affirmative action, but it would not be our last. Her college counselors assured Erika that her 3.3 grade point and hospital related volunteer hours would result in immediate acceptance to the incoming class. We were puzzled and she was devastated to receive notification that she was not accepted, however. When I called the admissions office of the nursing school to ask about the disparity of what Erika had been told and what actually occurred, I was informed that other things than grades, volunteer work and recommendations were under consideration. The admissions officer, Ms. Washington, told me that "demographics" were also taken into account. We discussed the situation with Erika's high school superintendent and he made independent inquiry. Shortly thereafter, Erika was then notified of her acceptance into the school. Ironically, when finally enrolled she noticed that quite a few candidates in her class had grade point averages lower than hers. Due to "demographic" features, they apparently met the admission criteria.

Although preference programs are marketed to the public as "opening the door" to under-represented minorities, the reality is that they close the door to others who have played by the rules and have worked to achieve the requisite grades, scores and qualifications that were said to be necessary for any given process. Happily, our daughter went on to successfully receive a Bachelor of Science degree in Nursing in the spring of 1997. Many family members attended her graduation ceremony. We were so proud to see her cross the stage to receive her diploma.

Initially, Erika decided to take work in sales for a medical supply company rather than do traditional nursing. This company, Cook Group, Inc. was the same one that employed my brother

Raymond. They specialized in catheter-based devices for radiology and cardiology, as well as other medical specialty applications. Erika joined the cardiology division, trained in Bloomington, Indiana, where the main offices were and eventually relocated to Minneapolis. She spent a couple of years calling on cardiologists in the Midwest and learned that it is not easy to sell things to people who do not want to talk to you or who were angry with the company you represent. Problems with her employer not filling back orders made her job as a field representative difficult. Nevertheless, this work opportunity allowed her to travel and visit many places, broadening her experiences as an employee and as a person.

Within time, Erika took a new position with another medical device company that made a special carbon dioxide adaptation for endoscopic surgery. This company asked her to relocate to Milwaukee in order to better contact and service gynecologists that operated in Chicago and Milwaukee. All of this work in medical supply and sales eventually made Erika realize that she did not enjoy being a saleswoman, especially when, so often, the prospective clients were not predisposed to speak with her.

In 2001, she decided to return to clinical nursing, taking a position with St Anthony's Hospital in Denver, Colorado. There, she worked on the maternity floor, which brought her to an area of nursing that she had always loved, contact with newborn babies. Prior to this time, she also had met Jim Harbridge, a young student from Wisconsin who was working on his PHD in Chemistry at the University of Denver. This love interest was eventually to culminate in marriage.

Parents of every generation rediscover, over and over, the truth that their children have a personality that is unique, even in their infancy. Many are surprised by this fact. Perhaps it is because there is a common expectation that children are primarily molded by the process of rearing, the result of which forms personality. Here, I refer to personality as those basic emotional and physical predispositions that an infant utilizes to respond to basic wants and needs and not to the more finished and learned aspects that I would refer to as character.

The erroneous cultural impression regarding personality results from faulty education about childhood development. I suspect that its origin is in the Enlightenment thinking of such men as Locke and Rousseau. They taught that the mind of the child was a *tabula rasa* or "blank slate" that was basically good and could be molded to benevolent purposes by society. Regrettably, this assertion has been the basis of much ill in the world. For example, this tenet was taken as gospel by the utopian disciples of fascism and communism. The adherents of *tabula rasa* continue to be in evidence in our current "therapeutic" approach to societal problems.

Thus, out of such bold theories emanates the parent's expectation that the child is an amorphous bundle that is simply waiting for our attention and input, parents who are oblivious to the fact that there is already much that is "hard-wired" into the computer. Without delving into concepts such as original sin and predestination, my emphasis here is on the simple presence of personhood in each newborn. In other words, there is something both divine and devilish about these little bundles that is waiting there for each sentient parent to see if they would just discard their preconceptions and look.

The contrast between daughter Erika and son Gabe was of this nature. One would have to obfuscate wildly not to be impressed by the differences between these two children from an early age. Even the obvious difference of girl versus boy carried much cultural baggage, some asserting that those differences are only due to child rearing techniques rather than biology. Frankly, there was nothing so clear to Kris and me that no amount of "gender neutral" rearing techniques would affect the predilections of these children. As much as Erika was feminine in her disposition and likes, Gabe was masculine.

However, the differences were more than gender related. Where Erika liked Dolls and tenderness, Gabe liked sports and action. Where Erika was verbal and talkative in her temperament,

Gabe was non-verbal and made his preferences known by gestures and not words. In this way, the common sense reactions of parents to their kids befuddle the learned child rearing experts. It may have taken Time Magazine to report the new research results to the public about gender and child development[77] but most parents received this news already.

Gabe was a remarkably physical child from an early age. I have still not run into any parent who recalls their child riding a two-wheeler bike, unassisted, short of their third birthday. This story began when Santa placed a two-wheeler under the Christmas tree, when Gabe was still two years old. From that moment on he badgered me daily to remove the training wheels from the bike. Every morning when I awoke, he stood at my bedside, staring relentlessly into my barely open eyes and asking me to "take the training wheels off". In March, when the snow had barely cleared from the streets, I finally relented, thinking it would be an impossible feat at his young age to learn how to navigate a two-wheeled bike. I expected the attempt would teach him the difficulty and would put the idea to rest. Imagine how surprised we were when after a few days and a determined, Herculean effort, struggling on his own, up and down the sidewalk in front of our house, he actually taught himself to ride!

It was that way with much that happened in the life of this boy. But while he was always physically advanced for his age, his judgment was not equally developed early on. For example, once when Gabe was four, our doorbell rang. A gentleman informed us that he almost hit our son with his car in the intersection near our house. Evidently, Gabe invented a game where he perched himself near the top of the sloped side street. When he saw a car proceeding up the road toward the crossing, he raced his bike downhill to beat the car through the intersection. We are forever grateful to that man who warned us of that dangerous situation.

Gabe was either going one hundred miles per hour or zero. When he was awake he never stopped his physical play which included a number of sports and conditioning efforts. The time or inclination to read for fun or leisure, in spite of our pleas to the contrary, would not evolve until he was a young adult and then almost with the same passion that he approached his earlier physical pursuits. He was a good student however, and even though academics were not his main attraction, he became his class Valedictorian in high school.

In his high school years Gabe was part of an unusual group of athletes including the class ahead of him as well as his own. Such a group comes only once in a long while in a small town like Iron Mountain. These boys grew into men by competing against each other over the years, plus they had the internal leadership to keep up the effort in season and out. They never took the easy way out and continually strived to improve as individuals and as a team. Having watched them prepare first hand, I can say that I have never seen anything like it before or since at the high school level. Their legacy eventually included a state championship in football, beating Manchester in the final game 28-8 in the Pontiac Silverdome. At Michigan State University, in the same year of 1993-94, the same group of athletes lost in the semifinals in basketball, after being up by 17 points in the last quarter. Dual state championship trophies eluded the Mountaineers that day with a late game surge by Orchard Lake St. Mary's High School. Gabe was the varsity quarterback for three years in football and he was in his junior year during the state championship run. For four years he competed on the varsity basketball team, which also included the state semi-final run. He remains the all-time leading scorer in basketball at Iron Mountain High School.

It was remarkable that a group like these young men brought so much pride and happiness to a community like Iron Mountain. People from the town and surrounding area followed them closely at the games and in the press. Obviously, sports and athletic competition was a great past time for our community and this was nothing new. Starting in 776 B.C. and continuing every four years until they deteriorated under Roman rule in the fourth century A.D., the ancient Greeks had Olympic Games to honor their God

Zeus The Games were then revived in the 19<sup>th</sup> century and continue until the present with many of the same contests or events that existed in the ancient world. Clearly, high school competition is not the same as Olympic competition, but I draw the comparison only to illustrate the similarities for a people and a community regarding successful athletic contests. The success of the high school team in a small town has its corollary in the pride and unity that comes from the successful professional teams for the people that live in a city; again acknowledging the obvious differences between them. However, the fact that the high school competitor is not paid, in many ways, elevates his effort from the cynicism of the college and professional world in the public mind.

A downside to all of this exists in the personal sphere as well as in the greater public. Any fan of athletics has observed parents who are obsessive in their involvement with their kid's sports and activities. The father who repeatedly and publicly berates his child's performance or who undermines the team effort by coaching his child from the stands contrary to the coach on the sidelines is a common caricature. Similarly, the mother that plants the seeds of dissent in what should be a team effort or has unrealistic expectations of her child's skills is of equal frequency. Perhaps the behavior is motivated by the parent's attempt to capture their own lost moments through the life of their child. If so, the honest parent must strive to correct these excesses of vanity. Whether their children are involved in sports or other pursuits, at every point along the way, they must avoid living through their child. If they do not do this, then no matter how successful their son or daughter will be, something will be detracted from the final result.

Likewise, the fans in a community must endeavor to keep a healthy perspective on the importance of athletics. A game is only a game; it is not real life. A mature adult outlook in a community is necessary to give the proper message to the young athletes growing up in that town. The ancient Greek city states may have competed against each other in Olympic games on the plains of Olympus, but in the fifth century, B.C., when Darius I and the larger Persian Army invaded Greece they all came out to battle to defeat this threat on the plains of Marathon[78].

Interestingly, Gabe's passionate approach to competition kept my own perspective balanced. Because of his intensity in sports, I never had to pester him to practice or train. On the contrary, he was his own harshest critic and he was, almost to a fault, driven to prepare. Thus, I found my own niche as a supporter who could bring a wider perspective to the performances and offer an encouraging view. In fact, I was often a brake on his desire to practice and tried to keep him from overtraining. Many are the times that I came out to the basketball court beside our home, turning off the lights around 11 PM, sending Gabe to bed before he completed the last 100 shots and thereby sparing our neighbors the sound of a bouncing ball late into the night.

It was a tribute to the fine young men of that group, that when Gabe made his plans to marry, he chose them to be his groomsmen. That is, of all the good friends he had made from college, work and graduate school, he chose to have his high school team-mates and classmates stand up for him at his wedding. These four future groomsmen were Brian Pinks, Don Bunnin, Jess Larson and Bryan Schorman.

After high school, Gabe wanted to continue playing football at the collegiate level. He received many scholarship offers from Division II and Division III schools, but none from Division I schools. In spite of being named to the all-state football team and playing in the State of Michigan All-Star Football Game, he was still from a small school in a fairly remote area. Never one to shy away from competition, when he was offered a preferred walk-on status at Division I Colorado University in Boulder, Colorado, he accepted. By the middle of his second year there, Gabe had won full scholarship status and ended up playing five years as a Colorado Buffalo. He played under both Coach Neuheisel and then Coach Barnett at the positions of quarterback, safety and special teams during his career there.

His playing time at the collegiate level was never what his father thought was commensurate with his proven ability, but in that arena one finds that those decisions are beyond one's control. It is not sour grapes to assert that politics play a role, because they do. Like all things in life, however, Division I football was a learning experience for Gabe and one that has made him stronger for having accepted the challenge. Playing college football had many positive aspects which countered the occasional frustration and injury. Being part of a talented team of athletes, traveling to places that others only hear about, and meeting the personal test of high level competition were all pluses. Furthermore, Gabe was well-liked and respected by his team-mates and still has many good friends from those years. All in all, it was an exciting experience for Gabe and for all his family, and one that ultimately allowed him to earn a degree in mechanical engineering at the same time. He graduated in the spring of 2000, receiving his diploma during the commencement activities at the Colorado School of Engineering. Not many players on a Division I roster can boast of earning an engineering degree while they played. It is a tribute to Gabe's work ethic that he was able to manage academics and athletics together.

After a brief stint in sales in Denver, following graduation, Gabe accepted a position as a mechanical engineer in Chicago with Sargent and Lundy, an engineering company that specialized in power plant design in projects all over the world. Within a short time, he was sent to Corpus Christi, Texas, where the final construction phases for a gas-steam-driven power plant were underway. Gabe was the on-site company trouble-shooter there for over a year and had invaluable experience in all aspects of the start-up of that facility.

Returning to Chicago in 2003 he applied to the University of Chicago School of Business MBA program. With high test scores, satisfactory interviews and excellent recommendations, he was accepted into this competitive and elite school and began night classes while continuing to work for Sargent and Lundy. The courses in business school fostered an interest in finance and investment and resulted in a career change during this busy time in his life. Also, a friendship that began during Gabe's tenure in Texas subsequently flowered into a growing romance with marriage plans for the fall of 2004. Remarkably, Jeannie Messer, a native of the Chicago area, attended Colorado University at the same time as Gabe but never met him there. Through a mutual friend, they met in Chicago where Jeannie was studying for another degree, this one in nursing. In early 2004, she received her RN and began work as a surgical nurse with Rush-Presbyterian St. Luke's Hospital.

Son Zachary Charles was always his own person, just as his sister and brother were. His sociable personality was unique from the start. Because he did not sleep for long periods and breast-fed frequently, he was a demanding infant. Kris spent months back then suffering from sleep deprivation. She often said kiddingly that if she had Zach first it was not clear that she would have been eager to have the other two. Unlike his brother, he was a very verbal youngster, who spoke not only in sentences, but in paragraphs at a very young age.

Zach was very physical when playing, but fortunately he did not have the penchant for dare-devil antics like his brother. He was decidedly more cautious about risk taking. However, from the earliest time it was clear that he had an unusual and remarkable sense of humor. Zach apparently inherited the performance gene from the Leonard side of the family and the one-liner responses of his Uncle Chuck from the Erickson side. His dinner table comments provided constant entertainment for all of us. An interesting symbiosis between Gabe and Zach arose out of this fact.

Gabe was intense and serious by nature, whereas Zach was more laid back and entertaining. Erika was the mediating foil, who enjoyed laughing at both brothers' foibles indiscriminately. Little by little, Gabe began to emulate his younger brother and the result was that he became a better-rounded youngster who was able to laugh at himself and with others more easily. The change made him more accessible and easier to be around. On the other hand, Zach learned from his older brother a diligence of effort and a discipline of character, traits that were among Gabe's strengths. In this way both of my sons learned positive things from each other that mutually benefited them from there on.

Zach was also a superior student who succeeded in primary and secondary school without making a major effort to study. His high school grade point exceeded his brother's record and yet, in his class, that earned him salutatorian rather than valedictorian honors. In athletics, Zach had great expectations to fulfill in view of his brother's accomplishments, but he acquitted himself very well. Like his brother he played football at the quarterback position. In basketball he played successfully at the guard position. Zach did not have the same talented cast around him that Gabe did, but Zach learned much from his older brother's group, frequently competing against them and honing his skills as he did so.

In 1996, when Zach was in his junior year, he also quarterbacked his team into the state finals at the Pontiac Silverdome against the perennial powerhouse St. Martin DePorres High School. In the first half, with Zach's accurate passing, Iron Mountain had DePorres on the ropes. By the second half however, the bigger, stronger DePorres team pulled away to a victory 30-14. It was a unique honor for me to have had both of my sons quarterback their teams in the state final games. I feel fortunate to have had such an exciting time with them during their athletic careers.

Zach's focus on academics was greater than either of his siblings in the high school years. He heeded the advice of his older brother, who encouraged him to spend the necessary time and effort to maintain a high grade point. He did so with a degree of ease that was remarkable. He used his time for work and study well, thereby accomplishing much in a shorter period of time. This left him more than adequate time to be sociable. He enjoyed a full experience in extracurricular affairs and came within only hundredths of a grade point of the valedictorian position as a graduating senior. Zach has continued to be able to focus and to work extremely hard on his academics and, in a moment's change, to put just as much energy into his pursuit of fun.

While Zach enjoyed a normal childhood and young adolescent life, a significant health problem shadowed him during his adolescent years. Because he had a congenital chest wall deformity, I did a basic medical workup, which included an electrocardiogram, just prior to Zach's involvement in junior high school athletics. I was shocked when the cardiogram revealed the characteristic electrical changes of Wolff-Parkinson-White syndrome. WPW, as it is called, is a congenital abnormality of the electrical system of the heart where an extra, or accessory, pathway exists. This pathway can be associated with various tachycardias and irregularities of heart rhythm, some of which can be serious, or even fatal. Although Zach was asymptomatic at the time, his condition could become dangerous and a cardiac specialist recommended study and possible treatment. This form of treatment is done by catheter ablation of the extra (aberrant) conducting pathway in the heart[79]. Zach had several ablations at Sinai Samaritan Medical Center in Milwaukee before he entered high school and we assumed these were successful.

Just prior to his enrollment at the University of Michigan, Zach was asked to be a walk-on to the football team there. He was assigned equipment and a locker, and then reported for the required physical exam by the team physician. To everyone's surprise, this doctor suggested that Zach have further study of his previous cardiac condition before he could be approved to play at the college level. Fred Morady, M.D., a renowned cardiac electro-physiologist at the University Hospital, restudied his condition that fall. He discovered that a dangerous pathway had reopened, that, in fact, Zach "had a sword over his head". Thus, Zach underwent his 5th ablation treatment to remove this Sword of Damocles in November, 1998. Although successful, this put an end to his football aspirations. It was an unusually stressful freshman year, but Zach held up and continued his education in fine form.

Zach turned out to be a superior student at the collegiate level. In his junior year he was asked to become a member of the prestigious society of *Phi Beta Kappa*. He was one of only seven juniors in the college of Literature, Science and the Arts to receive this honor at Michigan that year, a school that numbers over 3000 students. His performance in several courses earned him high praise from the professors, who wrote glowing letters of recommendation for him for medical school.

His application to medical school after four years of college afforded us the opportunity to again view the process of affirmative action from a personal perspective. Michigan's medical school would not even offer an interview to this Phi Beta Kappa candidate!

Ironically, at about the same time, the University of Michigan's undergraduate and graduate schools were being sued in separate court cases that wound their way to the Supreme Court of the United States. The final decision of this court in June, 2003, was a 6-3 split decision which disallowed the admission process for undergraduates. This system had previously given 20 points, or one fifth of the total points, for entrance strictly based on race. The law school case was a split vote of 5-4. The decision in both cases endorsed a place for race as a factor in the admission process[80]. The latter case allowed "narrowly tailored" efforts to use race to achieve the "compelling interest in obtaining the educational benefits that flow from a diverse student body", as written by Sandra Day O'Connor in the opinion regarding the law school case. In finding a case for "diversity", a popular term in modern times but not one found in the language of the constitution, our Supreme Court once again gave preferences to some on the basis of color, race, ethnicity or gender (traits they cannot control) while taking away the fruits of the hard work of others (based on features the individual can control). The fundamental unfairness of this in regard to moral right or to the Equal Protection Clause of the constitution must await another court and another day.

Shelby Steele, who is a black writer and commentator, has written about " . . . the liberal notion that equality can be engineered by simply intervening to spare minorities from open competition[81]". He suggests that " . . . liberalism is essentially an apologia, and its appeal is that it gives American institutions a way to show remorse. It offers a double standard to minorities that symbolically matches the double standard of racism". The answer to this liberal fallacy, for those of us that perceive its sophistry, is not to run from the debate but to assert the facts boldly. "The least conservatives can do", continues Steele, "is to go after racial preferences like they mean it-in the spirit of intolerance for unfairness and distaste for the condescension to minorities that preferences represent." This is so well stated that I can say no more.

Fortunately, Wayne State University Medical School had no such compunction regarding Zach's application to their institution. They offered him not only a position in the incoming class but a preferred status with full tuition paid. This is not to say that WSU did not do much the same things in regard to preferences, since it appeared that all the academic programs seemed to march to the same affirmative action drummer. However, the difference in offerings to my well qualified son from each of these schools is of considerable magnitude. Clearly, Wayne State's offer was a deal maker. It was proudly accepted by Zach and by his father who, of course, was an alumnus of the WSU medical school. He entered with the class of 2006 and has done a commendable job in his first several years. He has put his sights on an orthopedic surgical residency after graduation.

At some point in life we all find the truth of the aphorism that "life is not fair". It is not that we need to accept those things that are fundamentally unfair when there is a way to change them. Where there is a realistic chance that our efforts will bring about a change for the better, it is our moral responsibility to do our best to bring it about. It is also important to sense when our efforts will be futile so we do not end up as *Don Quixote* "tilting at windmills". The role of the parent in these matters is to help his children confront life's obstacles and to find alternatives and ways to prevail even when the deck is stacked against them. All of my children have confronted such situations, as have I, but my pride in them stems from knowing that they adapted and succeeded in spite of the roadblocks that they encountered. This is what I referred to earlier as character. It is not innate and has to be learned. I am proud to have played a part in the development of such character in all of my children and have relished its further development as they grew and matured.

# CHAPTER 12

## THE 1990'S

The last decade of the 20<sup>th</sup> century was one of those occasional periods in our national life when the mood of the culture was one of self indulgence. In a republican and free country, citizens have the freedom to either pay attention to what is transpiring in other parts of the world or if they are not of necessity predisposed to do so, they may pretend that the rest of the world does not exist. I say pretend because the world is and always has been a dangerous place and those that chose to pay it no heed do so at their own and other's peril. The danger does not disappear just because we do not notice it. In fact, it becomes even more hazardous in our modern day of rapid travel and instant communication to merely tune out to the threats that are always there.

Most of us assume, perhaps subconsciously, that even if we are temporarily out of touch, our chosen leaders will stand in for us and monitor those threats that are present. Seen from this vantage point it becomes very important that we choose our leaders well. Of all the qualities of a national leader, perhaps fitness for protecting national security is the most important. The "shining city on a hill" cannot function if it is in serious peril. It bears on the character of these leaders that they will by nature fulfill this unspoken promise. Even in ancient or primitive societies the tribesmen expected that their chieftain was in touch with his sentries around the realm.

There have been other periods in our own history when the leadership was not up to the job and when the national mood was one of indifference. One could look back to the era after the Civil War when a weary nation had all it could do to rebuild the war-damaged infrastructure and to deal with the failed attempt at reconstruction of the south. Lincoln's vision from his Second Inaugural Address "to do all which may establish and cherish a just and lasting peace, among ourselves, and with all nations" was lost in the bitter wrangling over Andrew Johnson's impeachment after the assassination of our greatest president. Ulysses S. Grant, our 18th Commander-in-Chief, was a good battlefield general but not as good a president. His administration became mired in the scandals of railroads and banking during that restless time. An inward-looking public had no counterpart in positions of leadership to look to what transpired beyond our shores. Fortunately, the dangers from other places were then relatively small.

The period leading up to the First World War was another period when American inattention and neutrality did not serve us well. Our lack of focus gave way to the sinking of the *Lusitania* (1915) and other ships by German submarines and drew us into that conflagration later in 1917. Woodrow Wilson ran for president on a pledge to keep the U.S. out of the war and within four months of his administration we, in fact, entered the war; so much for campaign pledges. Although the "doughboys" brought an end favorable to the allies in the war, the aftermath of the Treaty of Versailles and Wilson's failing health resulted in a shaky peace with little American involvement, thus contributing to the German military buildup that would result in World War II.

In the interwar period, between the 1920's and 1930's, continued American isolationism along with British and French fecklessness led mightily to German rearmament and Japanese militarism. To be sure, we had economic boom times and then the Great Depression to keep our attention occupied, but the subsequent loss of 458,000 GI's in a war that quite possibly could have been averted suggests that we were slumbering while danger grew. The repeated pleadings of Winston Churchill to his British countrymen were well detailed in his first volume on the war entitled *The Gathering Storm*, which is a tragic commentary on these matters[82]. On our side of the Atlantic, our nation had its own problems with reality, as Japanese incursions in China and German blitzkriegs across Europe were largely disregarded right up until Pearl Harbor. In a speech to parliament in 1936, Churchill characterized the stark reality of the situation better than any other could. His words still stand as a challenge to all free nations that will not face up to their responsibilities in a dangerous world ruled by brute force:

> "Virtuous motives, trammeled by inertia and timidity, are no match for armed and resolute wickedness. A sincere desire for peace is no excuse for muddling hundreds of millions of humble folk into total war. The cheers of the weak, well-meaning assemblies soon cease to count. Doom marches on.[83]"

In contrast, at other times in our own nation's history, the national mood was similarly self absorbed, but good leadership protected us from barbarians outside the gates. Such was the period of the 1950's when Dwight Eisenhower was in the White House during the Cold War. The inward looking character of those of "The Greatest Generation", who after coming home from World War II set about to build a life for themselves and their country, was understandable. However, as I previously stated, the populace was fortunate to have a wise and capable leader like Ike at the helm who was in touch with his sentries around the realm, even though he gave the impression that he was also as detached as his countrymen. The sense of satisfaction and contentment of Americans at that time was heightened by their apparent knowledge that things were so under control that the president had only to worry about his golf game!

However, the latter part of the decade of the 1990's was an unfortunate concatenation of a preoccupation of the public mind with fairly trivial matters at the same time that our executive leadership was similarly self-absorbed. Before we consider the national soap operas that were subsumed under the names of O.J. Simpson and Monica Lewinsky, it would be good to look back to the early part of the decade and specifically to the period of the Gulf War and the subsequent presidential election of 1992.

The performance of the U.S. Military in Desert Shield and Desert Storm was more than exemplary, it was unprecedented. Saddam Hussein had taken Kuwait and bragged that any attempt to oppose him would be met by the "mother of all battles". Many in the U.S. Congress and in the chattering class predicted tens of thousands of deaths of American GI's if we were so bold to attempt a military effort to disengage the powerful Iraqi Military from Kuwait's oil fields. The standard charge was made that it was not worth American lives to fight a war that was "all about oil", willfully oblivious of the fact that the whole of the western world runs on oil and that an interruption of market forces to its acquisition would cause untold suffering for many.

Nevertheless, George Bush "41" declared that the action of Iraq's dictator "would not stand" and he made preparations to back up his pledge. He assembled an impressive coalition of countries and achieved UN acceptance of the narrowly tailored intention to eject Saddam from Kuwait. In retrospect, the objective was overly narrow since the real aim was to not only dislodge Saddam from Kuwait but to dislodge him from Iraq as well. This assertion was born out by the fact that even the subsequent Clinton administration declared in 1998 that Iraq's continued weapons of mass destruction programs necessitated "regime change" as a stated goal of U.S. action. This was duly seconded by congressional action which included virtually all of the Democrat critics of the later Bush "43" Iraq invasion. Unfortunately, in 1991 there was an unstated desire with a poorly planned objective, which assumed that if Iraqi forces were defeated in Kuwait, then Saddam would topple with his military.

But the action of the U.S. Military was nothing short of awesome in the battle phase that took place after the buildup of our forces in the Gulf and prior to the stated UN deadline for Iraq to withdraw from Kuwait by January 15, 1991. Starting on the 17th of that month a devastating air attack took out any effective Iraqi command and control systems and withered the morale of its fighting troops. When the invasion began on February 24th with an allied ground attack, an unprecedented collapse of the regular Iraqi army resulted in mass surrenders in the desert.

Within four days the enemy combatants were completely degraded and, largely as a political decision, President Bush declared a cease fire at 8 AM on February 28th. In the last day of the war the televised images of the "highway of death" showed numerous wrecked vehicles and dead people, who had been trying to escape Kuwait. General Powell thought these pictures of mangled heaps of metal stretching from Kuwait City to Baghdad, as a result of U.S. air strikes, detracted from the positive effect of the U.S. effort. He therefore advised President Bush to end the hostilities to maintain good public relations. When President Bush took his advice, the news of the victorious war effort was received with cheers and celebration in the U.S. This news was met with similar celebration in the Iron Mountain Leonard household, where we had been concerned for months about the safety of Marine Cpl. Raymond Peter Weaver.

There was no way for the public to know the negative consequences of the early close to the war at that time but with the perspective of the later Iraq war we became acutely aware of the downside. Obviously, Saddam Hussein remained in power at the end of the conflict, continuing his oppression and slaughter of his Shiite and Kurd minorities. He continued to thwart the efforts of the United Nations weapons inspectors and remained a destabilizing influence in the Middle East. Under the aegis of the corrupt oil for food program, we now know that Saddam was building funds to rebuild his nuclear and biological arsenals, with the complicity of some of our supposed "allies". His connection with radical Islamic terrorists posed a continuing threat to the West through the remainder of the decade and into the next. These latter assertions are under such a political microscope in the present day that it is tiring to argue the facts of the matter point by point. With the passage of time and beyond the short term election cycle of Bush vs. Kerry, the factual basis for them will likely become manifestly clear. Suffice it to say here that if Saddam had been removed from power after the First Gulf War then these issues would not be a point of contention today.

Many military historians have weighed in on the conduct and the outcome of the U.S. Military in the Gulf War. It certainly was not the "mother of all battles" as promised by Saddam and predicted by the pessimists in the west. American technological warfare and determination had no counterpart in the highly touted Iraq military. The faster, more accurate and longer-range U.S. armor outgunned the Russian-supplied, Iraqi tanks. The feared Republican Guard was soundly defeated. But Bernard Trainor, a retired Marine Corps general and New York Times military consultant, faults General Norman Schwarzkopf for misreading the battlefield, thereby allowing two thirds of the Republican Guard to escape back to Baghdad, thus reconstituting the repressive Iraqi military in the years ahead[84]. The so-called highway of death was actually littered with mostly stolen vehicles from Kuwait whose occupants actually abandoned them in the desert when air strikes began. Seen in this light, the advice given by Joint Chief of Staff Powell to call a halt to hostilities was very premature and erroneous. When the order for the halt went out, several of the field commanders were just ready to engage additional Guard units and were very upset at the timing of the cease fire. But being good soldiers they followed orders.

The lack of a clear plan for the denouement of the Battle for Kuwait led to years of continued military engagement and taxpayer expense in policing the "no-fly zones" and in monitoring a persistent hostile regime in an unstable region. Seen in the crucible of time, the current Iraq War is merely a final conclusion to a conflict that was left incomplete by the First Gulf War. The faults of the poorly negotiated, cease-fire talks at Safwan laid the stage for the later war just as Versailles did similarly for World War II. Once again, Trainor asserted that the Americans were out finessed by the Iraqi generals in these talks and the coalition victors of the war, in essence, lost the peace. To wit, Schwarzkopf tipped his hand, letting the Iraqi's know that U.S. Forces were not going to Baghdad, thereby taking away the trump card of apprehension that he had. Furthermore, he allowed Saddam's generals the use of armed helicopters which he mistakenly thought would be used to transport supplies. Instead, they were used to attack and put down the Shiite uprising. General Glosson, Schwarzkopf's chief air planner, was especially outraged by his ground commander's conduct at the Safwan conference[85].

Victor Davis Hanson, an American military historian and a professor of classics, has stated that the incomplete conclusion of the Gulf War was the biggest blunder that the U.S. Military has made since the mistake of allowing political influences to alter the prosecution of the Viet Nam War[86]. Decidedly, it was only after critical analysis and over time that these criticisms have surfaced. However, in 1991, directly on the heels of victory, the nation was in high spirits and had a unity that had not been seen in the era of Viet Nam and its aftermath. The Gulf War victory parade took place on June 8th in Washington, D.C. George H.W. Bush had made good on his promise to expel Iraq from Kuwait. He was riding a wave of popularity that was about as deep-seated as it was to be short-lived.

Given the short memory span that sometimes characterizes the American electorate, the good fortune of George Bush "41" faded by the presidential elections of 1992. The Democrats nominated a relative unknown, William Jefferson Clinton, the governor from the small state of Arkansas. He turned out to be a savvy campaigner, assembling a corps of spin men and advisers that outdid the less robust Bush team. The James Carville adage that "it's the economy, stupid!" transmogrified the discussion away from the successful war effort. By taking the heat off of the draft-dodging of Clinton, the Democrats parlayed the discourse to a topic where they appeared to be more in touch with the public.

Tell the big lie often enough and people will eventually begin to believe it. This maxim was first coined by none other than

Adolph Hitler[87]. Interestingly, the Democrats have, since FDR, been successful in painting themselves as the party concerned with the "little guy". In that vein, they painted Bush "41" as an Eastern Brahmin who did not know the cost of a carton of milk, whereas Bill Clinton did, thus making him much more in tune with the life of the "common man and woman". Moreover, Clinton campaigned as a relative conservative from a southern state and it was not until later that he revealed his liberal tendencies. It was a successful ploy and Bush was unseated in the election that November.

It is still amazing to look back on this election, contemplating that a president can be so high in the public mind at one time, then little more than a year later he can fail to be reelected. British Prime Minister Winston Churchill knew this lesson of republican government well, having been defeated by the Liberal Party in the parliamentary elections after WW II. Subsequently, when the King of England offered to confer Knighthood on him in 1945, Churchill was quoted as saying "I could hardly accept His Majesty's offer of the Garter when his people have given me the Order of the Boot"[88]. Eventually, he was granted The Order of the Garter by Queen Elizabeth in 1953. Certainly, George Bush "41", having experienced first hand the vicissitudes of democratic republican government, was presumably as amazed at the election of 1992 as anyone on this side of the Atlantic. *Sic Transit Gloria Mundi* (Thus Passes Away Worldly Glory).

Without Question, the early years of the Clinton administration refuted any speculation that he would keep his campaign promise to govern as a conservative Democrat. One of his early presidential pledges was to "lift the ban on homosexuals in the military". This provoked a fire storm in the military hierarchy as well as in conservative groups. Clinton then unveiled a tactic that he would use frequently and quite successfully throughout his administration and in his post-presidential years. Namely, he parsed and rephrased his policy either in his own statements or in clarifications given by his spokesmen so that the result was to soften the meaning or make the original policy or program more acceptable. This often resulted in a more ambiguous policy and thus less assailable by his critics.

In this specific case, Clinton's Secretary of Defense Les Aspin came out with a compromise proposal[89] that would "allow homosexuals to serve in the military as long as they keep their sexual orientation private". This eventually morphed into what Georgia Democrat Senator Sam Nunn, chairman of the Senate Armed Services Committee, had proposed as "don't ask, don't tell". This issue and its allied issue of women in combat, the first things out of the Clinton box, engendered distrust in the military for the commander-in-chief, a sentiment that prevailed for both of his terms of office. Ironically, Clinton deployed the military frequently during his tenure but the men and women in uniform never developed an essential trust or respect for him. During those years many members of the armed services were lost to cuts in the administrative budget or voluntary retirement by the disaffected.

The president often referred to the first lady as the "second president". He appointed her to chair a health care task force that became a focus of congressional and public inquiry. Shrouded in secrecy during its deliberations, this commission proposed a remake of the health care system, thus affecting 14% of the economy. This effort was commonly known as "Hillary-Care". As American citizens and congressional representatives became cognizant of the details of this sweeping, centralized, socialist transformation of American medical care, their concern deepened and most of the program ultimately went down to ignominious defeat in the legislature. Definitely, the American public was not going to have Washington, D.C. dictate their choice of physician and determine the extent of their care. The demise of Hillary-Care and the way it was managed from the White House left a taint on the future progress of the Clinton "agenda" and, once again, warned observers that Bill was not the conservative Democrat he had claimed to be.

The death by apparent suicide of White House Deputy Counsel Vince Foster, the firing of White House correspondence analysts and Hillary's sacking of the White House Travel Office were additional incidents that were handled poorly and left scars on this inept administration. The questionable use of personal FBI files by the White House, the disastrous outcome of the Branch Dividian compound standoff in Waco, Texas and the persistent scandal of the Whitewater investigation can be added to the list of events that diminished the credibility and effectiveness of the Clinton Administration.

Midway through the first term of office, at the midterm elections of 1994, the Republicans regained control of the House and the Senate. From that point on, Clinton had increasing difficulty with liberal agenda items and had to "triangulate" himself in order to accomplish either his legislative efforts or his re-election. Fortunately, two positive accomplishments during these years were welfare reform and the North American Free Trade Agreement (NAFTA). In the case of welfare reform, a broad majority of Americans favored some type of alteration of a system that had strapped generations into a cycle of poverty. For years, Clinton had said that he favored such reform. Nevertheless, several presidential vetoes of proposed reforms took place before a Republican majority and many Democrats forced him to sign the legislation into law as the Welfare Reform Act of 1996. It is a testament to the will of the public on this issue that their elected officials took this step when they did. Many other legislative efforts with less of a public mandate then and since have ended in stalemate (i.e.-appointment of federal judges by both Clinton and Bush "43"). In spite of the apocalyptic predictions of mass starvation of the underclass by the liberal intelligentsia, the reforms were generally agreed by most commentators to have been a change for the better, even though much remains to be done to open a new horizon for the persistent poor of America.

Concurrently, in June of 1994, the murders of Nicole Simpson and Ron Goldman in Los Angeles began a chronicle of investigation and subsequent trial that became part of pop-culture entertainment for many in the public, at the expense of the long-suffering families of the victims. The 24 hour "infonews" cycle had already come of age but reached new dimensions in this case. Curiously, the public became addicted to the mesmerizing televised images, from the famous slow-motion police chase of the white Bronco on the freeways to the strutting Johnny Cochran, pronouncing in the courtroom, "if the glove don't fit, you must acquit!"

Astonishingly, in the criminal trial, O.J. Simpson's bevy of lawyers assembled a parade of expert witnesses who successfully dissembled the evidence against their client, thereby providing safe harbor for a jury that was obviously predisposed to disregard the facts presented to them. Legal experts from across the nation provided televised play-by-play analysis for the public. In doing so, they illuminated the rationalizations that comprised the technique of "jury nullification" that was utilized by the Simpson jury. An unfortunate, modern addendum to jury deliberation, this procedure entails the blatant disregard of the evidence at trial and of the rule of law. The founding fathers certainly did not conceive of this innovation when they penned the guarantee of trial by a jury of one's peers in the Bill of Rights.

Perhaps there is a deeper moral lesson or edifying factor revealed by this entire sordid affair. Among other things, I was impressed by what the O.J. Simpson episode divulged about the state of race relations in this country. To wit, the jury in the criminal trial which nullified the evidence was comprised of nine blacks, two whites and one Hispanic. The second or civil trial, where Simpson was found guilty, was comprised of nine whites, one Hispanic, one Asian and one person of black and Hispanic ancestry. Significantly, in February of 1997, after the verdict of the civil trial, a USA TODAY/CNN/Gallup poll showed that although whites overwhelmingly agreed with the Jury's decision, only a fourth of blacks agreed. In contrast, while most blacks were sympathetic to Simpson a majority of whites said they were unsympathetic[90]. Taken in its wider view, the O.J. interlude revealed a contemporary public that was not only unconcerned with the dangerous things occurring in the world outside of our own borders, but also one that was deeply divided along racial lines within. Without doubt, the latter fault line still exists.

Only a year later, the news cycle turned to the subject of Monica Lewinsky. Allegedly, Bill Clinton had a history of affairs and infidelities dating back at least to his days as the Attorney General of Arkansas. Various women had come forth with stories that were titillating to the public, such as Gennifer Flowers, Dolly Kyle Browning and Elizabeth Ward Gracen. However, in the case of Kathleen Willey the allegations were of more concern because, if true, they were clearly not consensual. Even more troubling was the story of Juanita Broaddrick, who actually alleged that while he was the Attorney General, Clinton actually raped her[91].

Consistently, Clinton always, either personally or through attorneys and spokesmen, denied the charges of these women. Sources in the press informed the public that part of the White House team was actually in charge of "bimbo eruptions". It was an article of partisanship or gullibility as to whether any reasonable person tended to believe that Bill was telling the truth (thus all these women were lying) or not. Such arguments saturated the air waves throughout his presidency.

The allegations of Paula Jones, however, unearthed another relationship that was to be fateful for Bill Clinton. This involved the story of Monica Lewinsky[92]. When he was required to testify in front of a grand jury proceeding brought by Jones lawyers, he admitted under oath that he "may have been alone with Ms. Lewinsky a few times and that they exchanged modest gifts". Over time, as the story unraveled, as the evidence of the semen stained blue dress came to light, it became obvious that an intimate and fairly long-standing affair had taken place. It is important to note that, at the time of its onset Monica was an 18-year-old White House intern. Even forgetting the morality of this situation, under the newly adopted sexual harassment laws that were promulgated by the Clinton Democrat party and its congressional representatives, any other executive or administrator in the country would be sacked for such behavior. Bill's spin doctors argued that such punishment as sacking or resignation was unwarranted with respect to the President over something that was only about "private consensual behavior". They turned the tables and insinuated that those who wanted to seek retribution were only obsessed with sex themselves. *Touché, monsieur!*

After congressional oversight relative to Clinton's Grand Jury statements, subsequent charges were brought by the House Judiciary Committee, including four impeachment Articles. These were approved on a party line vote of 21-16. The House of Representatives passed Articles I and III on December 19, 1998 setting up an impeachment trial in the Senate. In this trial, the Senate acquitted Clinton of the first charge having to do with "willfully providing perjurious, false and misleading testimony" on a bipartisan vote of 45-55. On the second charge of a "scheme designed to delay, impede, cover up, and conceal the existence of evidence" the Senate again acquitted Clinton on a bipartisan vote of 50-50. Impeachment requires a two-thirds majority under the constitution[93].

Focusing on the entire period, it is a colossal understatement to say that the diversions of the 1990's, especially impeachment, distracted the public and the Clinton Administration from the rising terror threats from radical Islamists. As previously noted, the Iranian hostage crisis was perhaps the first of a string of terrorist attacks against U.S. and Western targets. Within a few years, on Ronald Reagan's watch in 1983, a suicide car bomb killed 241 Marines in their barracks in Beirut. However, the attacks became bolder and closer to home on the Clinton watch with the first bombing of the New York World Trade Center in February of 1993. With six people killed and 1,042 injured, this outrage was not as successful as planned by its perpetrators. Nevertheless, even though it was the first enemy incursion on American soil, it was treated as a law enforcement matter, resulting in a lengthy trial and eventual conviction of men such as Ramzi Yousef and Sheik Omar Abdel-Rahman.

In June of 1996, a bomb aboard a fuel truck outside a U.S. air force installation in Dhahran, Saudi Arabia killed 19 U.S.

military personnel and wounded 515, 240 of whom were Americans. Subsequently, the U.S. Embassies in Nairobi, Kenya and Dar es Salaam, Tanzania were bombed in August, 1998. Then in October, 2000, the U.S.S. Cole was attacked in the port of Aden, Yemen, resulting in the death of 17 U.S. sailors and the wounding of 39 others.

With the benefit of hindsight, it is obvious that radical Islam had declared war on America. However, no one in leadership in America connected the dots and declared war on radical Islam. The responses made during the Clinton administration were not the determined responses of a leadership that was on a declared war footing, but rather one of a legal-criminal approach, using investigations, trials and limited military actions. For example, in response to the Saudi Arabian bombing of the Khobar towers in 1996, FBI investigators were dispatched and a frustrating cat and mouse game was played with local authorities with no real resolution achieved. Then, in response to the Embassy bombings in 1998, 75 cruise missiles and 60 Tomahawk missiles fired from Navy ships in the Arabian and Red Seas, struck targets in Afghanistan and Sudan, with little evidence of significant effect on the terrorists responsible.

An earlier incident from 1993 revealed how the Clinton White House responded to terrorist threats. On April 14th through 16th of that year former President Bush "41" visited Kuwait to commemorate the allied victory in the Persian Gulf War. He was accompanied by his wife, two sons, former Secretary of state Baker, former Chief of Staff Sununu and former Secretary of the treasury Brady. A plot to assassinate Bush and his entourage using a bomb in a Toyota Landcruiser was discovered by Kuwaiti authorities and interrupted[94]. Soon after the plot was revealed, the Clinton administration sent FBI, CIA and Department of Justice investigators there. By June, they reported their conclusions to the President that Saddam Hussein was either directly or indirectly tied to this plot. After considerable discussion between the White House and its best national security advisors, a decision was made to launch a military strike on Saturday, June 26, 1993. On that night 23 Tomahawk guided missiles were fired from American Navy warships in the Persian Gulf and the Red Sea, striking the Iraqi intelligence service complex in downtown Baghdad. Unfortunately, three missiles went off course, landing in nearby homes killing eight civilians and injuring twelve others. Queried by reporters on his way to church services the next morning, Clinton expressed regret over the loss of life but added, "I feel quite good about what transpired. I think the American people should feel good."

The president chose to take the advice of his advisors, including his national security advisor W. Anthony Lake, when deciding to use this plan of attack. In subsequent newspaper stories about this decision, Lake was quoted to have characterized Iraq as a "real and present danger" in his briefing of the president. He counseled Clinton that "if we fail to act and act now, the Iraqis might continue attempting such acts of state-sponsored terrorism". Granted, some have questioned our government's case against Iraq in this matter. Seymour Hersh, in a lengthy article in 1993 appearing in The New Yorker[95], argues forcefully that the evidence was circumstantial and the suspects questioned were unreliable.

Nevertheless, if Clinton truly believed the evidence presented to him by his best advisors, why would he not have responded with more than a "Saturday night" missile attack in downtown Baghdad. In point of fact, does not the attempt to assassinate a former president of the United States warrant a more powerful attack, even a declaration of war? Alternatively, this question should also be asked of those who today criticize Bush "43" for having declared war on Iraq, a country that these critics claim was innocent of ties to terrorism and to Al Queda.

Clinton's response to the Kuwait assassination plot and to other terrorist episodes goes to the heart of the character of the man. Looking at his years in the White House and at the years since, it appears that Bill Clinton responded to the crises of his day with no clear grounding or compass but rather out of a sense of damage control. Consequently, he used the military frequently during those years, but with the possible exception of Kosovo, not often effectively. Thus, rather than fear her, America's enemies came to despise her. Those who paid attention to the statements of Osama Bin Laden knew that he considered Americans soft, unlikely to respond to further acts of terrorism with anything but a few bombs or missiles launched from a safe distance and with no risk to American lives. In a helpful comparison, the Senate Intelligence Committee's investigation of prewar intelligence on Iraq (i.e.-prior to the Iraq war of 2003) reported their findings in July, 2004. This report was anxiously awaited in the climate of recriminations that have come about as a result of 9-11. It stated that the (CIA) failures were a product of "a risk averse corporate culture"[96]. I would suggest that this culture typified not only the CIA but the entire Clinton approach to governing. The CIA was merely taking its cue from an administration that was in permanent "cover the backside" mode.

The response of the Clinton team to these criticisms has been defensive then and now. Hillary, in defending her husband during the Lewinsky scandal, complained that their agenda could not go forth due to intense opposition, which by implication, she characterized as more personal than political. She coined the querulous phrase that there was a "vast right wing conspiracy" mounted against them. Perhaps as an additional attempt to rescue a failed legacy, they have recently written extensive books, blaming everyone but themselves for their troubles. Hillary's book *Living History*, published in June, 2003, weighs in at 562 pages[97]. Bill's book, *My Life*, was unveiled a year later and comprises a withering 1008 pages[98]. Even former White House aide Sidney Blumenthal put his efforts forward in May, 2003 with *The Clinton Wars*, an 822 page[99] screed of self justification and pillory of everyone else. Certainly, there will be others. Omitting the likelihood that any of these people actually authored these tomes rather than managed a team of writers and spin-meisters, it seems obvious that a lot of explaining is needed to answer the simple question, what happened to the Clinton presidency?

To answer, consider a brief sojourn into the physical world. Newton's first law of thermodynamics is the law of energy conservation. It says that energy cannot be created or destroyed. It can be said that energy expended in one system is not available for work in another. By analogy, presidential power follows a somewhat similar law. There is only so much time and energy that the chief executive has in his years of office. If a good deal of effort is expended in damage control and in more inconsequential ways, then less is left for substantial accomplishments on behalf of the American people. Whether they want to admit it or not, the Clintons brought about their own troubles and can blame themselves for the lack of progress toward their goals. Whatever any of us think about these matters, history will sort out the final judgments. My own opinion is that the results will not be kind to them.

# CHAPTER 13

## MARRIAGE IN THE FAMILY

There are many joys which accrue to parenting but few match the satisfaction that comes from the marriage of a son or daughter to the right person. However, the choice of the "right" person is something in which the parent has little, if any, input since arranged marriages went out of vogue with the passing of Victorian Europe. With respect to the learned process of character development in raising children, this is where the most important aspect of this learning is tested. Surely, as with most choices in life, character matters greatly in making the proper decision.

Aristotle felt that character is by its nature related to virtuous activity. In the *Nicomachean Ethics* (II.7) he defined virtuous character:

> Excellence [of character], then, is a state concerned with choice, lying in a mean relative to us, this being determined by reason and in the way in which the man of practical wisdom would determine it. Now it is a mean between two vices, that which depends on excess and that which depends on defect.

The key aspect of this definition is that character is a habit of choosing between extremes using reason, linked to virtue. The assertion that character is a practiced and learned behavior implies that the parents are intimately involved in its development in their children. Properly nurtured, their character will then support them in the important decisions of their lives as they grow into maturity.

If our children have this basic foundation, their decisions will consequently be the best that can be expected. Once they have learned those aspects of character from the proper and guided choices of prior experience, they will subsequently be ready to make this crucial choice of a spouse on their own. Specifically, once character is instilled in the individual, that individual will recognize character in others. The sharing of hopes and aspirations that is crucial in marriage will devolve from this mutual recognition in the partners. Thus, parents should not feel at a loss in not being involved in the marriage choices of their children. Taking into account the variable nature of human development, in most instances the parenting role has set the stage for the "right" choice. I felt assured when daughter Erika and son Gabe told us of their wedding plans and I am sure that is how I will feel when Zach informs us of his plans for marriage. Confident in my children's character, I knew and still know their choices will be right.

Choosing the right marriage partner is important because both must share their dreams together, they must value raising their own children together and there must be love between them. However, from the larger societal and human standpoint, it is the proper raising of each generation that matters most. The mutual attraction that brings a couple into matrimony is sanctioned by society in greatest part because of its interest in the progeny of that union.

Interestingly, over the millennia of human history, men and women have experimented with various types of childrearing plans. In ancient Sparta, men and women lived separately and sons were separated from their parents early in life to live in dormitories devoted to military training. Young girls also were separated to train for the raising of future hoplite warriors. In ancient Persia, many of the women and children lived in the harems of the wealthy rulers of the land. In the Old Testament, King Solomon was said to have had 700 wives and 300 concubines. Edward Gibbon, his famous book *The Decline and Fall of the Roman Empire* tells us of Emperor Gordian the Younger that:

> Twenty-two acknowledged concubines, and a library of sixty-two thousand volumes attested the variety of his inclinations; and from the productions which he left behind him, it appears that both the one and the other were designed for use rather than ostentation[100].

For some time during the 19th century, polygamy was practiced by the Mormons in our present state of Utah. A free love, communal colony called New Harmony was set up in South-Central Indiana in the early part of that same century. In the 20th century, in the Soviet Union, families were broken up to form the collective farms. In Israel, the kibbutz was tried for a time. A former first lady of the U.S. has even written a book that asserts that "it takes a village" to rear children.

Of these many experiments in child-rearing, the great majority in our present day have decided that the best way to raise children is in a family with one mother and one father. This societal norm is not written on stone tablets or depicted in the formation of the stars, but nonetheless, as the product of man's slow development throughout the millennia of history, it is tested and true. The marriage of a man and a woman is agreed upon by people in our culture based on their prejudices and intuitions and as such has been codified into law. Academic studies also confirm these intuitions but most people do not need the academy to tell them what they already know in their hearts. It is for the optimal raising of children that makes the institution of marriage so important for the continued success of our culture. It also defines the importance of the custom of marriage and why "one man, one woman" should be protected and enhanced by our laws and norms. Seen in this light, marriage is about raising children.

The culture wars of the present day include pitched battles over the definition of marriage. Many feel that marriage should be redefined to include other arrangements than the traditional one of a union between a man and a woman. Other arrangements between consenting adults are possible, but in the majority opinion of most Americans, marriage means one man, one woman. Currently, President Bush is proposing a constitutional amendment to protect traditional marriage because some in black robes and in positions of authority, against public sentiment and legislative will, have redefined marriage in their own way. It is too bad that it takes such a drastic measure just to allow the public mind to assert itself.

My preference is to have the definition of marriage decided state by state, through the elected (state) representatives of the people. Thus, if a state decides to change the standard for the recognition of marriage, that should be their prerogative. Unfortunately, using the principle of equal treatment under the law and the commerce clause of the constitution, the advocates of gay marriage want to force the recognition of gay unions in one state onto other states that oppose that proposition. Given these ploys, there may be no other way to protect the dissenting states than to place wording into the federal constitution that was never anticipated to have been needed by its founders.

Having looked at the broader, societal significance of marriage, it is time to address the title of this chapter, "marriage in the family". For Erika, wedding plans came after several years of courtship, which began with a first introduction that was specifically not encouraged by her younger brother Gabe. This occurred when Gabe hosted a party at Colorado University, during a time when Erika was visiting him. Jim Harbridge, who was originally from Wisconsin and who was also working on his PHD in chemistry at the University of Denver, was traveling to this party when a mutual friend, Ryan Dishnow, warned him that Gabe did not want anyone to "hit on" his sister. According to Jim, when he first saw Erika, he determined that he could stay awake longer than Gabe, providing him the opportunity to "hit on" Gabe's sister.

A long-distance relationship ensued but was made difficult by Erika's sales job and her travel around the Midwest. When she decided to go back into clinical nursing, she moved from Milwaukee to Denver. There she took a nursing position in the labor and delivery department of St. Anthony's Hospital in downtown Denver. A closer and romantic relationship developed. They announced their engagement at my mother's 80th birthday celebration at our Spread Eagle cottage on July 4th, 2002. The wedding was scheduled on the Labor Day weekend of 2003. Since the entire Leonard family was present at the announcement, everyone anticipated the chance to come together and celebrate with them in the coming year.

Prior to their wedding, Jim finished his research and doctoral thesis, receiving his PHD from University of Denver in the spring of 2003. He was offered a position with Hach Company, a water technology company in Loveland, Colorado. With Jim and Erika both employed, they were able to afford the purchase of a new home in Thornton, Colorado, that summer. Jim, a fun loving guy, enjoys sports and hanging out with his friends. He is smart, but without ostentation, almost to a fault. His dry sense of humor keeps Erika entertained, as does his quick-witted approach to life. From my perspective, humor in particular seems to defray much of the tension that may arise from time to time between husband and wife. From a parent's standpoint, it is heartwarming that Jim and Erika have a respectful and loving relationship.

As the wedding date approached, the planning of the ceremony and reception continued with Erika and Kris in frequent contact. It became increasingly helpful to Erika that her mother was able to attend to so many of the details of the event that she, living in Denver, could not. Erika had asked Kristina Santini, the daughter of our good friends Jane and Dr. Dennis Santini, to play the piano preceding and during the service. Kris and I spent several enjoyable nights at the Santini home reviewing and choosing the selections that Kristina would play. At the wedding she also accompanied Erika's cousin Chuck Erickson, who sang several vocal arrangements. During their rehearsal for the wedding, young Chuck's musical talent was instrumental in coordinating the pieces that combined the piano, cello and voice. Kristina and Chuck's performance was outstanding. Many who attended the wedding ceremony especially complimented their rendition of "It's a Wonderful World".

It was very meaningful to us that Pastor Richard Milford officiated at the service and in the same church where he married Kris and me 34 years before. Pastor Cowan and the support staff of Our Savior's Lutheran Church in Iron Mountain were very supportive in the change from the usual wedding protocol at their church and we were very appreciative of that. Many remarked that they were moved by Dick's personal, timely and thoughtful words to Erika and Jim during the ceremony. Our sons Gabriel and Zachary accompanied Kris down the aisle to her seat; it was a moment that brought tears to my eyes. Erika was a truly beautiful bride and, in traditional manner, I was able to escort her down the aisle without any missteps or emotional disturbances, having improved on my performance of 34 years earlier.

In so many respects this was a family and friends affair. Erika's cousin Dr. Joshua Leonard and her brother Gabe read elegant selections from the book of Ruth ("wither thou goest . . .") and the book of I Corinthians ("love . . . bears all things, believes all things, endures all things . . ."). Her cousin Kara was a beautiful Bridesmaid; son Zachary and third son Peter Weaver were handsome as Ushers. Erika's Matron of Honor was Heather Hiatt (DeGroot) and Jim's Best Men Ryan Dishnow and David Ramshack. The church was decorated tastefully with Kris' help and with flowers hand-picked by her good friends Michelle Carlson and Via Thomas. It was a truly lovely service.

Holly and Jeanne Dixon and Sue Bouchey, my dear friends and employees, were generous enough to have a cocktail party following the service at Holly and Ross Dixon's house near the church. The out-of-town guests and family members enjoyed the sunny, warm day out on their deck until the reception started. The helpful staff of the Premier Center made the planning and execution of the reception a remarkable event. Kris' detailed plans paid off as the hall was transformed into a beautiful wedding setting with almost an electric atmosphere. The food was great, the dinner wines of white and red Cotes-du-Rhone enjoyable, and the table seatings were perfect. Attention to detail seemed to enhance everyone's experience.

As the father of the bride, I had for some time considered what I would say during the toast to the married couple at the reception. In fact, I had formulated my remarks long in advance of the date and had rehearsed them frequently during walks and other quiet times. I had some apprehension of my ability to say what I had planned without overweening emotion. We all know ourselves and what propensity we may have for this, so thus I knew I needed some effort to control any excess sentiment. Good preparation turned out to be my best ally.

Years earlier, Erika and I had shared a special affection for the poem, "A Red, Red Rose", by Robert Burns, the 18th century poet Laureate of Scotland. Therefore, I decided to recite that poem at her wedding with some introductory remarks as well. To ensure the proper Scottish pronunciation, I worked with my friend Lee Ward, a pharmaceutical representative, who in his college years majored in Old-English Studies. Under my own poetic license, I made only a slight change in the last stanza, reciting it thus:

> O my luve's like a red, red rose,
>> That's newly sprung in June;
> O my luve's like the melodie
>> That's sweetly played in tune.
> As fair art thou, my bonnie lass,
>> So deep in luve am I;
> And I will luve thee still, my dear,
>> Till a' the seas gang dry.
> Till a' the seas gang dry, my dear,
>> And the rocks melt wi' the sun;
> O I will love thee still, my dear,
>> While the sands o' life shall run.

> And fare thee weel, my only luve,
>> And fare thee weel awhile!
> For I will come to you, my luve,
>> Though it were ten thousand mile[101].

In my introductory remarks, I spoke of the changing historical position of the father of the bride in choosing a spouse for his daughter, the need for love in the marital relationship and about how Jim and Erika seemed to have the requisite love that is needed for a successful marriage. I considered the opportunity to speak at my daughter's wedding reception a great honor and one that I still remember with joy and satisfaction.

Beyond our expectations, the first year of marriage was a blessed one for Jim and Erika. The birth of Ava Kristine Harbridge on August 6, 2004, became the highlight of that time. At 6 pounds 12 ounces, with curly brown hair and blue eyes, this small beauty continued the line of the next generation of our fortunate family.

The wedding of son Stephen Gabriel Leonard and Jeannie Elizabeth Messer was consummated on Labor Day weekend, 2004. As previously noted, these two "star-crossed lovers" came to that stage ironically, each having attended Colorado University at the same time but not meeting each other until they both lived in Chicago. Jeannie was from the Chicago suburb of Prospect Heights, where her parents James and Martha Messer still lived. She returned to Chicago after graduation to teach Spanish for a year. At the end of that time she found that she did not enjoy teaching as much as she expected and redirected her career into nursing. After successful completion of her nursing education, she accepted a position as a surgical nurse in the same hospital where she trained, Rush Presbyterian-St. Luke's. It is of note that her brother is a surgical resident at that hospital and she sees him fairly frequently during his many hours of surgical call. The Messer family is close-knit and Jeannie keeps in touch with her parents, her three brothers, her sister and all their families regularly.

It was previously noted that, as a mechanical engineer for Sargent and Lundy, Gabe spent time at a power plant in Corpus Christi, Texas. He had met Jeannie prior to leaving and they kept in touch increasingly during his work in Corpus. Jeannie even came to Texas to visit him on more than one occasion. Somewhere along the way, their friendship evolved into romance and love. They spent more and more time together after Gabe returned to Chicago and at some point began to plan their future together.

The decision to marry was announced in February, 2004, and was planned around Gabe's work and education demands, as he proceeded into his career change. Once Jeannie's nursing career was more certain, the wedding plans went forward and were scheduled around Gabe's semester break. Working full time and going to business school at the University of Chicago in the evening program kept Gabe a busy young man prior to his wedding. The redirection of his career into finance and investment prompted the decision to enroll in school full-time after the wedding, in order to complete his degree by spring, 2005. The sooner time horizon allowed Gabe to be more competitive with the needs of prospective employers during the ensuing interview process. Gabe found the MBA program at University of Chicago to be competitive and demanding but the strengths of that institution were exactly what he needed in his new field of endeavor.

The tight career demands on Gabe and Jeannie made the wedding plans difficult to schedule and the short time line left little available space for the service and reception. Thus, the entire festivity took place at her parent's home in Prospect Heights on September 5th, 2004. This "garden wedding" occurred just off the back deck of their home in a tastefully arranged "chapel", decorated with flowers and complimented by Jim Messer's gardening skills. Pastor Dave Wardle, a family friend to the Messer's, officiated at the service, carrying out his duties exceptionally well. Many were intrigued by his personal touch, especially when he recited the words that each partner had used to describe what qualities attracted them to their mate, words each had used previously during their pre-nuptial counseling sessions. Although he was a guest at the wedding, Pastor Dick Milford did not participate in the service there.

September 5th was a beautiful, balmy fall day in the Chicago area, one perfect for Gabe and Jeannie's garden wedding. The planning and execution of this pleasant affair was a concerted activity by the whole Messer family. Jeannie's brother Steve and Gabe's sister Erika did readings for the service, her brothers Tom and Jim were ushers, as were Gabe's brother Pete Weaver and cousin Luke Leonard. Jeannie's young nephews Jason and Alexander were Ring Bearers. Her sister Susan was Matron of Honor, sister-in-law Joy a Bridesmaid and Gabe's brother Zach was Best Man. A large tent/canopy served as a wedding hall for the dinner and reception in the sizable back yard of the Messer home. In the tableau of my mind, the wedding celebration that day was like watching two honorable Roman families, each coming together in tribute to their offspring.

The Hilton Hotel in nearby Arlington Heights served as the site for the rehearsal dinner and for out-of-town guests. Here we were first treated to a special DVD musical and photographic production of the lives of Jeannie and Gabe, produced by Rico Belluomini, brother of Jeannie's sister-in-law Joy Messer. A professionally done creation, it was an emotional and beautiful walk for us all down the memory lane of these newly-weds.

For Kris and me, the attendance of so many of our family and friends was particularly gratifying. My mother Emma Leonard, my Dad's sister Lorraine Vollnagle and her husband Jim and Kris' Aunt Claire Johnson were especially honored guests present. It is a testimonial to the quality of our family and friends that so many made the trip to Chicago, some from considerable distance, to be with us for this pleasing event. In conversations over the weekend, it appeared that the happiness of the moment was its own reward for them as well.

It is with delight that I observe Gabe and Jeannie making their life together. They have a tender and loving relationship and they share a hope to build their own family at some point to come. They are both mature beyond their years and their plans are well grounded in reality. Currently, they are living together at Gabe's residence, at 425 Wellington in the Lincoln Park area of the near north lakeshore of Chicago. Jeannie continues to work her nursing job, which she enjoys very much and in which she has had excellent recognition already. Gabe continues to work toward his MBA degree while preparing for the first part of the certified financial analyst exam and interviewing for new employment. I could not feel more proud of them both or more assured that they will make all of their dreams come true.

There have been other marriages in the Leonard family and there will certainly be more in, conceivably, the not too distant future. I have already referred to the marriages of my two physician nephews from the Clyde and Susan Leonard family. Josh Leonard found a perfect soul-mate and mother of the latest Leonard addition (Samuel) when he married Sarah Shasteen. Their wedding and reception took place in the spring of 1999 in Sullivan and Charleston, Illinois, respectively, and was a great family get-together. Luke Leonard married Brenda Haberman in Port Orchard, Washington in 2000. Again it was a happy time for the Leonard family. My mother, Emma Leonard, has attended all of her grandchildren's weddings thus far and with God's help will be at the remainder of those to come. In this regard and at this writing, the marital plans of Kara Leonard and Zachary Leonard remain enigmatic, although hopeful possibilities abide.

The chapter on marriage in the family would not be complete unless it includes Pete Weaver's marriage to Lisa Marie Cerasoli in September, 2003. After returning from the military, Pete worked several jobs and eventually went back to school. He was to father a son with Tanya Edwards at that time and although they were not married, they mutually determined that their son would not grow up having only a mother or only a father. Brock Louis Weaver was born September 29, 1994. He grew into a precocious child and wise in the ways of the adults around him. Although his mother and father never married, he had the benefit of both parents and their extended families as he grew. In Peter's life Brock became the most important focus of his attention and a driving force of purpose for him. I would say the same is true for Tanya.

Pete found that he had a special talent for relating to kids and especially troubled kids. He worked for a degree in special education and took a teaching job in the Iron Mountain school system at the middle school level. His talent for kids and for sports was especially revealed in his coaching of ninth grade boys and girls basketball. He is able to communicate a sense of intensity and to bring forth the best effort his players can muster. He is well respected by players and parents alike.

In another of life's turns, both Pete and Lisa were thrown together by the illnesses of their fathers which occurred almost simultaneously. Both Jack Weaver and Dick Cerasoli were diagnosed with lung cancer and in the year 2003, the disease progressed in both men. Lisa had been living in Los Angeles, writing screen plays and a novel, and acting in the daytime drama "General Hospital". She and Pete had known each other since high school but it was to be their fathers' condition that brought them closer. Lisa returned to Iron Mountain to help in the care of her father. Pete's father, who lived in Marquette, Michigan required more of his time as well. The bond between Pete and Lisa became more firm as time progressed and they decided to marry in September of that year, hoping that Jack's failing health would allow him to be present. Unfortunately, Dick died in June and then unexpectedly, Jack developed a mortal infection and died in August, depressingly short of the hoped for day.

Under these circumstances, the wedding was a bittersweet affair. It was held at Lisa's family home in Iron Mountain, outdoors on a sunny, warm late September afternoon, in the fall of 2003. Given Lisa's flair and creativity, it was a beautifully planned affair and a good start of much happiness for them both. Brock, at age nine, was the best man for his Dad and did a stand-up job in that capacity. The Cerasoli and Weaver families were present to celebrate this marriage in the midst of their grief. The Iron

Mountain Leonard family was present to see their third son and their grandson take the vows of matrimony. In spite of the forgone adversity, it was a happy day.

It is unfortunately true that families tend to come together most often and even solely at weddings and funerals. Modern life being what it is, things are too hectic and the members spread too far and wide to allow many of them to be present at other times. The decision to marry is momentous for the couple to be wed, but also a happy occasion for the family members that will travel to be present when the vows are taken. Along with close friends that will attend, the wedding ceremony is a remarkable event that cements the bonds of the entire family heading into the future. It stands as a landmark of pride to all that attend and a point of reference for the bride and groom as they make their life together.

# CHAPTER 14

## MARRIED LIFE AFTER KIDS

I t is a truism of most marriages that once the children are gone, there is a period of adaptation that comes to husband and wife in their changed circumstances. "The empty nest syndrome" is probably different for each couple that encounters it, but there is a commonality of some loss and a need to adjust to each other anew. Kris and I had the benefit of being eased into these changes by the gradual shifts that occurred as each of our offspring left for college and work.

Pete's stint in the Marine Corps was good practice for what was to come. Erika's years in college were counterbalanced by the busy years of high school and the athletic careers of her brothers Gabe and Zach. When Gabe left for college the distance from Iron Mountain, Michigan to Boulder, Colorado signaled a more decisive shift in things to come. Zach, the last one in the nest, used his singular place in the family to good benefit over the intervening years. His penchant for a busy social life meant that much activity accompanied his time at home and even at the times of his school breaks. It also meant that when Zach and his entourage departed the abrupt change around the house was greatly perceived.

As the pace of activity in our home dwindled with each departure, it left more quiet time for Kris and me to fill. Because we shared the basic feeling that raising our family is one of the most important things we do as human beings, we found ourselves increasingly preoccupied with thoughts and plans surrounding our now more distant kids. Phone calls, letters, e-mails all served to keep us in touch with those lives that still meant so much to us. Plans to visit, then preparations to have them back home for a time filled our lives with expectation and superseded whatever loss we felt. Inevitably, like all parents in similar circumstance, we also needed to confront what effect, if any, this change may have had on our marriage together. Some couples, facing an "empty nest" together, would agree with Hamlet: "Ay, there's the rub".

The Merriam-Webster Online Dictionary defines empty-nest syndrome a "the emotional letdown experienced by an empty nester". The Yahoo search for this term turns up 76,100 sites and Amazon.com has 19 books relating to this title. One begins to wonder whether our self absorbed society is making too much of something that all other generations have faced as a normal life process, only lacking the time and resources to obsess about it the way we do?

Certainly, in many cultures throughout history and ever since men and women have made families, children have left the home of their parents to make their own way. In the short history of our own country, the "emotional letdown" of this separation was considerably different for earlier generations of Americans. The young immigrants who departed from their native lands to sail on ships to the land of opportunity often left their parents and families behind, never seeing them again in many cases. The mothers and fathers who saw their sons enlist in the armies of the Civil War or in the great wars of the 20th century must have experienced more than an "emotional letdown". However, it is unlikely that they described their feelings in the same popular therapeutic parlance of our time. With many of us now facing less momentous separations, perhaps we have over dramatized these landmarks in our lives.

Nevertheless, it is important to make the adjustment that is needed in marriage without wandering into a permanent nostalgia or an overactive refusal to let the grown children get on with their lives, free of constant parental oversight. This transition is more easily made if husband and wife have a pre-existing marital life that is built on personal love and respect. It is also essential to have good friends with whom to share life's vicissitudes. I think Kris and I met the personal criteria well. Our friends met this test equally well. Dennis and Jane Santini, John and Therese Fortier, Jay and Kathy Dishnow Gary and Via Thomas, John and Myrna Schon, Jim and Kris Andes, Paul and Nettie Santoni, John and Nancy Daley, Don and Terry Summers, Peg Schram, Carl and Tammy Smoot, and (last but not least) the faithful ladies from my office were but a few of those that personified Aristotle's idea of friends of pleasure, but also often exceeded to the level of friends of character.

Kris and I were not only husband and wife, but we were lovers and friends. The importance of our mutual friendship was crucial in keeping us together even when our most important protégés moved on. It is fair to say that we were each other's best friend and reciprocally regarded ourselves in that way. Not infrequently, there have been things that I thought of or read about which seemed too personally focused or too narrow to discuss with other friends or associates. The particularities of one person's conceptions often appeared inappropriate during friendly social conversations. These things always have had a willing and able ear in my beloved wife. I have cherished the chance to speak with her on such occasions and to get her feedback in relation to them. In similar fashion, she felt she could confide in me.

Alternatively, a husband and wife should be able to enjoy many of those things in life which are apart from their own marital relationship. Many times, edifying work and play is best done separately rather than exclusively together. Early in our marriage we came across Kahlil Gibran's passage from *The Prophet* that counseled:

> "For the pillars of the temple stand apart,
> And the oak and the cypress grow not in each other's
> shadow.[102]"

Remembering this truth as we have gone forward, we neither require nor begrudge those activities that, in moderation, take us to disparate realms for a time.

The simple fact of the matter is that men and women are different and only understand each other incompletely. Thus, men sometimes enjoy the company of other men and the inimitable activities they share. Most women have the same inclinations. For example, in leisure time, among other things, I enjoy camp life and working on construction or wood cutting projects. Having a scotch and smoking a cigar with the guys is a relaxing camaraderie. On the other hand, Kris plays cards with her group of friends who call themselves the "mad dogs", or simply enjoys a night out with the "girls", shopping or dining. Such quotidian but separate things keep the temple standing.

Ineluctably, the importance of family and friends cannot be underestimated. Because family members are often scattered geographically in our time, the role our friends play becomes considerable. John Locke and other natural law theorists have posited that "man is by nature a social animal". The inclination to form friends and then groups of friends is thus a natural activity from which we derive pleasurable experience. Aristotle, in the 4th century B.C., regarded this natural tendency to associate together to be the basis by which men formed the natural political unit he called the *polis,* or city[103]. In fact, those men that were not inclined to associate with others or to be part of the *polis* he characterized as "either a mean sort [beast] or superior to man [God] . . ." Apart from their political meaning, friends are our primary assist in how we become more complete people.

Social interaction with our friends is something Kris and I have enjoyed and continue to enjoy. The occasion to get together may be a daylight or evening cruise around the Spread Eagle chain of lakes, a quiet dinner at each other's home, attendance at a motion picture or an informal gathering around a roaring campfire. The possibilities have been numerous and protean. At these times, men and women have overcome our basic misapprehension of each other (we only understand each other incompletely), using that wonderful and God-given gift called conversation. Whether the discussion might be abstruse or trivial, it has usually been punctuated with laughter and often encouraged with wine and spirits.

Wine, in particular has been an avocation of mine. I have enjoyed collecting wines from the various regions of the world and sampling its many characters and flavors with friends. Wine is "civilized" in the best sense of the word, since it has been around since men and women came together in civilized societies. It is almost impossible to drink wine without commenting upon it. Thus, it lends itself to convivial discourse. What a versatile symmetry it provokes! Wine has also provoked many to speak and write of it throughout history. In Ecclestiasticus: 31:27; "what life is then to a man that is without wine? For it was made to make men glad[104]". In Shakespeare's *Othello* there is the admonition; "Come, come; Good wine is a good familiar creature if it be well used; exclaim no more against it[105]". Without a doubt, between us and our friends, we have often been made glad with wine, although possibly not always was it well used! All of our friends have enjoyed bringing their latest acquisition to be mutually savored and there has been a place for everyone, whether well-versed collectors of the beverage or novices. In these circles, there has been no place for wine snobbery.

While personal and social aspects of life evolve after the children leave the family nest, a third aspect, possibly the most important, is the work that we do. In the best sense of the word, our work denotes activity that fulfills us and that precedes, accompanies and then follows the raising of a family. It allows us to provide something of value to others in our community in exchange for the value they repay to us. Consequently, a husband and wife who have a good marriage as well as the benefit of good family and friends are still particularly lacking if they do not have the mutual consummation provided by work.

In the Declaration of Independence Thomas Jefferson penned the "inalienable rights" of men to be "life, liberty and happiness". These rights are bestowed by God and not by man and hearken back in history to those natural law proponents discussed previously. Again from Aristotle, whose prolific writings covered almost any subject that bears discussion, comes the relevant thought. The Greek word for happiness is *eudaemonia* and it means something quite different than we usually suppose. Rather than a state of feeling good about oneself that we may conjure, Aristotle's use of this word in Greek denotes "the main universal goal, derived from a life of activity governed by reason"[106]. It is the active life and not the contemplative life that is crucial here. That the activity is directed by reason is equally important. This is the sense that Jefferson invokes in our founding document, and I submit that it is one's work to which he primarily refers. Work, by its nature, involves the active life. Aristotle and Jefferson, among others, place it as the main, not subsidiary, goal of our existence. Work then is, by no means, subordinate to the other things we do here on earth.

Although the medical profession is one of the oldest of mankind's activities, changes in not only the technology but also the practice of medicine have accelerated in the latter decades of the 20th century and into the new millennium. Consequently, interesting changes have occurred in my own work over the 28 years of medical practice. Early on, I chose to study and practice medicine because of a desire to use my skill and learning to help others in need. In addition, traditionally the healer's role allowed for a high degree of personal independence and satisfaction. However, the independence of the physician has diminished considerably in the period in which I have labored.

In my profession, regardless of the form that the health care delivery system conforms to, the sense of privilege that the physician experiences in being chosen to serve the patient is significant. Thus, personal satisfaction will always derive from the interaction between doctor and patient. Furthermore, the trust of the patient in the physician underscores the caretaker's need to maintain the confidentiality of that trust. Hippocrates implored us to "not divulge" what "in connection with my professional practice . . . I see or hear, in the life of men". To this interaction, the physician brings his skill and learning to help the afflicted individual. When successful treatment is possible, both parties share its benefit. Even when medical science cannot provide a cure, the physician can still help to relieve pain and alleviate suffering. The wise counsel of the physician can also help the patient avoid untested or ineffective treatments ("first do no harm"). In this way, there will always be satisfaction in being a physician.

The practice of internal medicine, by its nature, is a branch of medical care that involves older and chronically ill individuals in the majority of cases. The elderly suffer the accumulated effects of the diseases of aging such as heart failure, diabetes, emphysema, and cerebral vascular disease. Also, although certain cancers target children, the majority of malignancies afflict primarily the aging population. In our modern day these older individuals are covered by the umbrella of the various rules and payments of the Medicare system, a government-run monopoly, which has a "one size-fits all" approach to patient care and the financing of that care.

Physicians who treat patients over age 65 are at the mercy of this system and its permutations. My desire to be independent meant that I envisioned treating patients in a much more individual fashion than has been allowed during my practice years. I did not realize going in that I would become more or less a government-employed physician, following the mandates for care and confined to the charges for my services promulgated by the bureaucracy. One of the main problems in this day of procedural medicine is that so-called "cognitive care" is remunerated poorly. Specialties like internal medicine involve primarily "cognitive care" as the service provided. Thus, as the reimbursements are cut and the costs of practice increase, most new primary care physicians join larger organizations in order to survive the system. A private practice like mine is something of a dinosaur.

Medicare started out as a well-meaning effort by government to help senior citizens pay for their costly medical care, knowing that the last years of life are when the bulk of health care expenditures occur for most individuals. Unlike Social Security, Medicare is not financed with funds set aside during the working years of the recipients, but rather it is paid by the younger working members of society at the time the retirees need it. Like most government entitlements, it has grown to unpredicted expense. Furthermore, as the Medicare population has become inured to the payments and pronouncements of the system, they have in subtle and some not so subtle ways become entitlement captives. What was started as a taxpayer gift to a remarkable generation of American seniors has become an ever enlarging budget buster for younger working people. When, for example, the politicians talk of expanding that gift into a drug benefit, many seniors reflexively counter that whatever plan is contemplated, it is not enough!

This has been an unfortunate development and it is a major argument against expanding this system into some European model of universal health care for all members of society. The siren song of government give away, with no effort to means-test for the recipients in greatest need, is nothing but a lure to the leveling control of the welfare state. It will take the ship of state to the shoals and rocks as sure as it did the ancient mariners returning from Troy.

In spite of these health care financing issues, the daily challenge of medical practice and its satisfying aspects keeps my interest in my chosen profession high. The rapid pace of technological development in medicine is daunting and the individual presentation of diseases is humbling. When I was in medical school one of my professors estimated that the science of medicine changes thirty per cent every ten years. The challenge to keep up with newer information is stimulating. Continuing education whether reading or meetings, is important, but of greater importance is that the physician constantly re-examines his skills and offers further consultation when appropriate for care or even for the patient's peace of mind.

An integral part of my ability to deliver timely and excellent care relates to the quality of my long standing and loyal office staff. Their attention to detail and their warm and savvy approach to people has been a remarkable complement to my practice over the years. My patients know that they will receive professional and personal attention from my staff and many just stop by the office to talk to them or, in some instances, to show pictures of a new grandchild. Holly, Susie, Sherry and Jeanne are certainly like family to me and I enjoy greatly the camaraderie that we have together.

When I started out as a newly-minted physician in 1976, I was much more involved in hospital-based and acute-care medicine. This was a product of my training and a need that I could fill as the only boarded internist at the county hospital. As the years have passed and more sub-specialist physicians have been added to the staff, I have backed off of hospital based care somewhat and done more in long term and outpatient care. My practice is less procedure oriented than previously and more cognitive than before. I have enjoyed this transition since I am now more involved in the prevention of disease and in office management to prevent acute complications rather than treatment of far advanced and uncontrolled problems. I still fill a need for my patients who become acutely ill and require my services in the hospital setting, as well as for those of my associates when I am on call. However, overall the volume of acute work has lessened.

In 1990, it was an honor to be appointed to the hospital board by the Dickinson County Board of Commissioners. In conjunction first with Marvin Dehne and then subsequently with John Schon, both able administrators, our board brought to fruition the planning and construction of a new county hospital. Many people worked diligently to complete this project and I am proud that all of our efforts resulted in a ground breaking on November 11, 1994 and a grand opening on November 10, 1996. As a result of these unyielding efforts, the citizens of the Dickinson County area, including the adjacent counties from northeast Wisconsin have a first-class health care facility that will serve them well into the 21$^{st}$ century. It is almost impossible to look back and imagine how we functioned in the outdated old hospital on Woodward Avenue or what our medical care would be like now without the new inpatient complex and its adjacent medical office building, located on a sizable campus on US 2. I am honored and proud to have been part of this effort during my tenure and after eight years on the board I chose not to seek reappointment in 1998.

Throughout our marriage Kris has been the financial handler in our relationship, managing the home front expenses while the kids were growing up. She also was closely involved in managing my practice expenses. When accountants met and advised us, as much as possible I wanted her present, since I valued her perspective on the personal and the professional in this regard. After the death of her mother Muriel, Kris began to fill in as the receptionist in my office. She covered for vacations and illness in that capacity. After the kids left for school, Kris became increasingly involved in the business side of my practice, doing much of the accounting and bill-paying.

During the winter of 2003, Kris decided to venture into another career, in addition to her functions in my practice. Having been interested in real estate for a long time, she took the required real estate courses for the State of Michigan and passed the test for licensure. She postponed her actual entry into the business until after Erika's wedding, so it was not until mid-November, 2003 that she signed on with the Stephens GMAC Real Estate Agency. By the spring of 2004, she had her Wisconsin license also, thus she was able to list and sell homes in the entire area. With her new responsibilities in real estate and the demands of my office book-keeping, Kris is indeed a busy woman. As the end of the summer of 2004 approaches, with a new grand-daughter now born and a son recently married, I am sure she would say that she is even busier than she wants to be. *C'est la vie.*

# CHAPTER 15

## EMBRACING CONSERVATISM

A t some point in the 1970's I began to suspect that my education had been defective. This is not in reference to my schooling in science and medicine or even in literature, all of which seemed to be reasonably sound. It was, of course, in those subjects that most of my formal education was concentrated for reasons of career and interest. Instead, it was in respect to history and political economics where the fault line emerged into my consciousness. Relative to either American or world history I had to admit a general dissatisfaction with my grasp of things. In being truthful with myself, I could see where the lack of a solid familiarity with those subjects had led to the adoption of a number of sophistic explanations of how the world was constituted. Some of this is discussed in Chapter 6—"Leftist Politics".

Actually, my formal schooling in these things had been reasonably good for the period in which I grew up. If we can believe the present day studies on the dismal knowledge of many high school and college students about history and politics, I probably would have seemed fairly erudite by comparison. However, the era of the educators of my time was the first to substitute "social studies" for history and "civics" for government in the classroom. Thus began a progressive drift in the teaching of the factual details of history to a softer emphasis on concepts. Rather than learn about archaic dates and long-dead people we were encouraged to "get the big picture" and to concentrate on the "broad themes" of the past and present. Realizing that history is not the same as math, it would nevertheless shock us if a math teacher were to ask his students to locate the constant *pi* somewhere between 0 and 10! However, these trends have led to the present day students, of which we hear, that cannot locate the civil war within 50 years and are uncertain of whom fought on the side of the Allies in WWII. This type of squishy background in history and economics leads to faulty logic when it comes to one's reasoning in later life, and I began to sense that about myself.

It was Mark Twain who said "Never let mere schooling get in the way of your education". Once I began to perceive the defect in my own schooling, I set out to remedy the situation, as best I could, with the enthusiasm of an autodidact. The repair process and the full realization of what was missing came in small steps, each leading to a larger journey of discovery. It was initially the microcosm of American history and government that showed me the way to other realms.

Our founding fathers, who signed the Declaration of Independence and pledged "our lives, our fortunes and our sacred honor[107]" on behalf of this new republic, first occupied my attention. Why would they risk their lives and their fortunes in such an effort and what did they plan to accomplish? It had to be more than a tax on tea that motivated them. By comparison to our present taxes, the tea tax is virtually dwarfed. Conversely, the answer to this question cuts to the basis for much of the enmity of the culture wars of our day.

Certainly, our founders knew that they had a unique opportunity to form a government in which free men would choose to allow themselves to be governed in a way that protected their freedom for the future. Rule by "the consent of the governed" was unheard of in previous history. Their grievances against their former rulers were sufficient and the time was then right. Vigorously, they set forth to "dissolve the political bands" of their former tyranny and to construct a new form of government as though their lives depended on it. King George III made sure they understood the latter in a bloody and ultimately unsuccessful attempt to quell the American insurrection. Subsequently, how the founders knew of their unprecedented chance to accomplish their task speaks directly to their own education and wisdom, and it also speaks to the issue of "American exceptionalism".

In great contradistinction, one of the most tiresome terms of the present day culture wars is the concept of "multiculturalism". This politically correct phrase connotes that there is really no difference in the ways that people around the world have come to socialize and govern themselves and that we should not judge one culture as better than another. Multiculturalism is the antithesis of the idea of American exceptionalism because the latter term, by its nature, judges our way of life to be better than the others.

The American founders knew however that what they were involved in was better than what went before and it was not merely because of partisan *hubris*. Rather, because they were educated enough to know the discrepancies of all the past attempts of men to govern, they tried mightily to avoid similar mistakes at our founding. On the back of the dollar bill near "The Great Seal of the United States" is the Latin phrase *Novus Ordo Seclorum*. The American republic was to be "a new order for the ages". To the chagrin of the multiculturalists, this phrase announces our founders' intent to the entire world. What was the evidence that their claim was correct?

When the delegates to the constitutional convention had labored and argued and compromised to produce our constitution, it was recognized that much resistance persisted in the public to its acceptance. Having won a costly war against the British to free themselves from tyranny, many Americans were still wary of substituting a new federal power in its place. Ratification of the document by the states was thus not assured, by any means. Alexander Hamilton recognized the need to sell the constitution to the public and enlisted James Madison and John Jay to help in writing a series of essays explaining the background and rationale for the proposed constitution. These articles were published widely in newspapers at the time under an anonymous author called *Publius*. Publius Valerius had laid the foundations of the Roman Republic after the overthrow of the monarchy and had been chosen by the authors as a suitable pseudonym.

Eventually, this collection of 85 essays and about 600 pages of text were published, in book form, under the title of *The Federalist* in 1788[108]. Hamilton, who was 31 years of age at that time, wrote the bulk of them. Madison, who was 36, wrote about a third and Jay at age 41 wrote five. I give their ages to emphasize their relative youth in years in relation to their great education and wisdom in matters pertaining to the previous efforts to govern mankind. One cannot be anything but impressed in reading Federalist no. 18 where Madison (and possibly also Hamilton) discusses in great detail the failures of the ancient Greek confederacies that resulted in the destructiveness of the Peloponnesian war and the ultimate downfall of the Greek city states at the hands of Alexander the Great.

Equally impressive is Federalist no. 69, where Hamilton makes a detailed comparison between the proposed presidency of the United States and the monarchy of Great Britain. With extensive analysis he is able to show that the tyranny of the unchecked hereditary power of the King is avoided by the elected and constitutionally-bound president. Consequently, the chief magistrate of this new republic was eligible for election "as often as the people of the United States shall think him worthy of their confidence".

The breadth and depth of knowledge of the men who called themselves *Publius* were unquestionably instrumental in the ultimate acceptance of the constitution by their contemporaries. Their writings were widely read and discussed in the public prior to passage. Their wisdom was matched by others of our founders and any reading or research of such men as Thomas Jefferson, George Washington or John Adams will confirm that assertion. The document they all produced should continue to command our respect and reverence today.

The educational attainments of these men were stimulating to me. The idea that the founding of our republic was unique and unprecedented was well buttressed by their writings. Additionally, the prominent place of religious belief in their lives and in the public square was noteworthy. The first amendment to the Constitution did not prescribe "freedom from religion" as many now insist but rather proscribes that "congress shall make no law respecting an establishment of religion, or prohibiting the free exercise thereof". In comparison, the Biblical covenant that God had with Israel, that they were a chosen people, was similar to the assertion on the part of the founders, that we were a chosen nation. Assuredly, a covenant implies a responsibility not only on God's part but also on the part of men. Thus the implication held by many, that our great nation had a mission to act with virtue in the world in order to deserve God's favor. The idea of American exceptionalism thus had both political and religious implications and I became more of a disciple of that creed as time went on.

From the founding, I moved forward to study the era of the civil war and, in particular, the person of Abraham Lincoln. With respect to exceptionalism, Lincoln was the *sine qua non* of an exceptional republican leader. His humble beginnings and subsequent success point to the unequaled opportunity that exists in this, the land of opportunity. I was particularly struck by his admission to his biographer John L. Scripps that his education was "defective". Certainly, being a kindred spirit to President Lincoln could not be a bad omen for me. In his second short autobiography he said; "The little advance I now have upon this store of education, I have picked up from time to time under the pressure of necessity". Scripps said of him;

> Abraham now thinks that the aggregate of all his schooling did not amount to one year. He was never in a college or academy as a student, and never inside of a college or academy building till he had a law license. What he has in the way of education he has picked up.

As I read of how he set about to repair his deficit, I found it marvelous and inspiring. He read and studied widely from sources as varied as the Old Testament and Euclid's geometry. He had an amazing capacity to remember things that he came across; Herndon, his law partner, said of him that his mind was like "steel". Once an item was written onto it, it was there to stay and could not be scratched off. Lincoln was the epitome of a self-educated man and the results of his effort are obvious to posterity He developed over time a unique speaking style. Many of his speeches stand as the best examples of "prose poetry" that I have ever known. I have engaged myself in memorizing some of them, such as the Gettysburg address and The Second Inaugural Address, and on certain special occasions, have even recited them to family and friends in my "A. Lincoln" dress costume.

Knowing that in my early lifetime, I had been predisposed to regard America as not being "exceptional" in comparison to other peoples and other times, the study of our great founders and leaders forced a personal re-examination of my previous views. I had been schooled in the forerunner of multiculturalism and was led to believe that the properly educated elite maintained a certain "objectivity" and "skepticism" of American motives and of American history. We were warned that "My country, right or wrong", was what Good Germans thought when they turned their back on the Holocaust. It was said that blind patriotism was not the stance of a properly educated person. Even at the time of our founding, Samuel Johnson, the Englishman, cautioned that "Patriotism is the last refuge of a scoundrel"[109]. After all, was not America the same nation that had sanctioned slavery, decimated the Native Americans and dropped the atom bomb on Japan? Furthermore, these concerns among the modern-day multiculturalists have additionally morphed into a trilogy of sins composed of racism, sexism and classism.

The multiculturalist critics of America cleverly compare American achievement against America's ideals. In this way it is always easy to point out that we fall short of the perfect. Interestingly, they almost never compare America to other places in the real world, either today or in history. Their litany of complaints against "America the Beautiful" was a tide that was hard to swim against, but nonetheless one that needed to be turned. Unhappy with much of this simplistic rhetoric, I knew I needed to get a broader view of the American experiment. I felt that the way to do this was to go back in history to the roots of Western civilization and then come forward again to the present.

To understand our nation's beginnings, I needed to be more conversant with the Bible. The Bible was not meant to be a history book but our culture is so intertwined with Biblical reference and meaning that its study is crucial. The Old Testament takes us back to the origins of Canaan, the Promised Land, and the first Patriarch Abraham. His sons Isaac and Ishmael are the said to be the progenitors of the Jewish and Arab peoples respectively, and so his personage has interest for the understanding of the Arab-Israeli conflict of the present day.

The figure of Jesus Christ is the single most written about individual in history. I could not understand the concepts of individual freedom and individual worth, which are taken for granted in our land, without knowing more of the life and teachings of this great and sacred man. It is equally important to understand the power that millions, over the millennia since his death, have derived from their faith in his ultimate Resurrection. Also, how his early followers came to compile the canonical books of The New Testament is a story that needs to be learned by any serious student. Studying the interaction of Christianity with the Roman Empire and then with the later Holy Roman Empire of Europe provided me further understanding of our own origin as a nation and as a culture.

Next, I turned to the study of the origin of our democratic and republican ideals of government as practiced by the Greeks. Our founding fathers were very conversant with Greek history and Greek culture, as I have noted. At one time a "classical education" included not only a historical and philosophical inquiry of this period but also the learning of Greek or Latin language. The demise of classical education is an unfortunate consequence of schooling in modernity. Ancient Greek culture begins with the mythological epics of the poet Homer. His classical texts, written after 500 years of oral tradition, the *Iliad* and the *Odyssey*, are the accounts of the Greeks and the Trojans in the Trojan Wars. Many present day references in literature and politics take their origin from characters from this period. Any medical student knows where the Achilles tendon is located but few know much about Achilles the warrior and how he was brought down by an arrow shot by Paris, the Trojan, striking him in his only vulnerable spot, the "Achilles heel".

The work of other writers of the late fifth century, B.C. or the "golden age" of Greece, are of interest to read in understanding more of this remarkable culture. Herodotus is recognized as "the father of history" and in his *Inquiries* he gives the rich background for the Persian Wars. Anyone trying to understand the origins of the present day clashes between Western and Middle Eastern societies would benefit greatly from reading Herodotus. Thucydides, with his *History of the Peloponnesian War*, describes the devastation of Greece caused by this internecine conflict which went on for 30 years. The way that the unexpected consequences of war come back to haunt the participants and how war, once started, can progressively brutalize society, is aptly described in his account. Those who lament the "quagmire" of Viet Nam or who harp on the mistaken intelligence that led to the Iraq War would be considerably better discussants by reading Thucydides.

Greek philosophy is fundamental to the understanding of why republican and democratic forms of government came into being in that era. The Greeks had a tragic view of life that accepted the flawed nature of human beings. Thus, men were not gods and they could be corrupt and barbaric if tempted by circumstance. Conversely, they were capable of virtuous activity only when restrained by the laws and the customs of the *polis*. Furthermore, human nature does not change over time. The forms of government developed by the Greeks accepted that basic view of men and women and specifically were designed to maximize the good in society and restrain or punish the bad.

Interestingly, our founding fathers shared much the same view of mankind as did the Greeks 2500 years earlier. James Madison said in *Federalist* No. 51, "If men were angels, no government would be necessary". The drafting of a written constitution indicated the desire of the founders to "form a more perfect union, establish justice, insure domestic tranquility, provide for the common defense, promote the general welfare, and secure the blessings of liberty to ourselves and our posterity". The narrowly tailored document they produced was designed to restrain the tyranny of government power and allow the exercise of those God-given "inalienable rights" by men. Anarchy and even the softer form of modern day libertarianism was eschewed by the Greeks and by our founders.

The Greek view of life differs greatly, however, from the modern day therapeutic approach. This contends that what some call evil is only a product of bad circumstance and can be expunged through the proper treatment by the various agents of society. Thus, society and government can counteract what appears to be evil using egalitarianism and fairness just as the counselor and therapist can treat mid-life crisis by getting the patient in touch with his inner self. Not so with the Greeks; they saw life as tragic and short and that men struggled against these hard facts and their own nature constantly.

A corollary to the tragic view of the Greeks was their world view regarding human conflict. Because men and the nations that lead them are corruptible, war will occur and combat will be forced on the protagonists. The pre-Socratic philosopher Heraclitus said that war is "the father of all, the king of all". That war was inevitable to the Greeks because of the nature of mankind, was born out by the written histories of Greece given to us by Herodotus and Thucydides, as previously discussed. In fact, if one reads history from any period apart from the Greeks it becomes obvious that war recurs regularly. In large part, history is essentially about the history of war.

Greek city states prepared for war and fought among themselves and with outsiders regularly. They developed a unique and brutal type of war in which a phalanx of hoplite warriors many rows deep would clash head on with an opposing army. Most often, the outcome was quickly determined and consequentially the victors took the spoils in slaves and treasure and the losers faced death and servitude. Unlike some in our present time, the Greeks had neither the hope that peace could be negotiated by experts in conflict resolution, nor would the United Nations come to their rescue. There was no "peace process" that was interrupted by the "cycle of violence". In their eyes, only by the maintenance of a strong military and the continuous training of hoplites could a possible foe be deterred. Somewhat later in history, the Romans had a saying; *Qui desiderat pacem, preaparat bellum*; Let him who desires peace, prepare for war.

The last aspect of Greek philosophy that I will discuss pertains to their view of the nature of truth; namely, are truths relative or eternal. In 5$^{th}$ century Athens, a group of Greek intellectuals arose, known as the sophists, the most prominent of which was Protagoras. They espoused a relativistic view of life that was at odds with the traditional Greek absolutist view. They were skilled at rhetoric and had followings of students who paid handsomely to learn to take any side of an argument and debate it cogently. Plato and his teacher Socrates spent a good deal of their professional lives defending the traditional view that truth was eternal and not relative to circumstance. These questions posed by the Greeks over two millennia ago are still with us today, only the participants in the debate have changed their names. We need only open our newspapers and read the opinions of the participants in the political issues of the day (i.e.-partial birth abortion, the death penalty for murderers, pre-emptive war, euthanasia, etc.) to see that as much as things have changed, they have really stayed the same. The word sophistry has acquired an unsavory connotation today, meaning something unsound or misleading, yet clever. However, the modern relativists still ride forth under that banner.

I have spent some time discussing the Greeks because they are important not only to me but I think they are important to us all. They have framed the arguments and asked the questions that we are still trying to answer. My own study of these people and of this time in human history has been of immense help in my own search to correct an educational "defect". I have seen, in our founding fathers, the effect of this influence and how Greek ideas were utilized in sculpting our own form of government. It is unfortunate that our schools no longer spend substantial time in studying this interesting civilization[110]. We are all made poor because of it.

Continuing forward from the Roman period and the middle ages, I paused to consider the age of the Enlightenment. This period preceded our own country's founding and provides much of the grist for the mill of our modern times.

The medieval ascendancy of the Catholic Church was questioned by Martin Luther and by the establishment of the Anglican Church during the Reformation of the 17th century. Francis Bacon's experimental method and Isaac Newton's discoveries of the laws of physics at the same approximate time served to promote the celebration of the powers of human reason. Philosophers such as Rousseau and Voltaire expanded on these developments and promoted a doctrine that asserted that people are capable of achieving perfection on earth given the right milieu and circumstance. The idea of man's perfectibility, resulting from the Enlightenment thinkers, again contrasts to the opposing tragic view of man promoted by the ancient Greeks.

The clash of ideas produced by these new forces as they battled with the more traditional thinking had real world consequences that have resonated to the present day. An understanding of these opposing camps sheds light on the two great political "revolutions" of the late 18th and early 19th centuries. The revolution fought by our fathers against King George III was led by men who were old line thinkers and who prized the freedom and order of constitutional democracy. They were not trying to throw off all law and tradition, but merely to throw off the tyranny that subverted it. Following our own, on the other side of the Atlantic, was the beginning of the French

Revolution. This was led by men who, enamored of the idea of perfectibility, dreamed of an entirely new order where all the old was to be thrown out and where man was to reach a new "natural" state.

A study of the contrasting nature of these cross currents leads to a fuller appreciation of the "conservative" revolution fought by our forebears. As a result of our separation from the England of George III, our founders established a stable form of government that has, with some severe tests, lasted over two hundred years with the same constitution. On the other hand, the revolution fought in France resulted in a series of horrors, including the murders of the royal family and executions on the guillotine of large numbers of French noblemen, clergy and others that were considered enemies of the movement. As the violence of the mob escalated, even partisans of the early revolt were judged later to be enemies. The government passed from Robespierre and the radicals to the Jacobins and into the Reign of Terror.

Since then, France has had no less than six constitutions. From the reign of Napoleon to the course of the 20th century previously discussed, the history of the French since their revolution has been, in many ways, lamentable. The lessons imparted here, especially in relation to the perfectibility hypothesis and its logical outgrowth, related, in particular, to the later revolutions of communism and fascism in the modern era. Thus, ideas arising from the improper assessment of human nature have had severe historical consequences. A more realistic and traditional view of humankind (the tragic view) might have spared much misery.

Many conservative thinkers have commented on these matters and some have been of particular help to me. John Adams, early on, saw in the French Revolution an inauspicious event unfolding. In his frank and cantankerous, New England way, he was more clear-minded about it than his contemporary, Thomas Jefferson. Edmund Burke, a British politician at the time of our founding, perceived plainly and wrote forcefully about the dichotomy of what was transpiring in America and in France. Burke, like our founders, was a well-read, well-educated man who heeded the ancients and Christian religious thought in his statements about the moral order. From him came the idea that Providence had taught humankind a collective wisdom through the trial and error of thousands of years of experience and meditation. Because men were fallible and not perfectible, the individual is foolish, but the species is wise. He was fond of quoting an earlier writer, Richard Hooker:

> The reason first why we do admire those things which are greatest, and second those things which are ancientist, is because the one are the least distant from the infinite substance, the other from the infinite continuance, of God[111].

Russell Kirk, a 20th century conservative writer and thinker, has written about Burke and other modern conservatives. Kirk's writings crystallized my own concurrence with conservatism, putting into words many things that I knew, somewhat by intuition, were right[112]. The idea that conservatives see in history a process of revelation from the Divine has been an insight that has helped me correct the defect that I started out to remedy. From this vantage point, the study of history became, for me, more than a catalogue of the foibles of mankind. To be sure, many oddities have occurred throughout history; but if that is all that catches one's attention, then perusing history is akin to reading a trashy novel. If, however, history tells us something about what God has imparted to men, then there should be and can be a certain reverence to its study. Without wanting to overstate the case, history offers something serious to us. In trying to understand those of the past, we may come to understand more of ourselves and of our relation to God.

A potential downside can occur when looking at history in this way. In concentrating on the great thinkers and leaders of the past, some aspects of the present may seem to pale by comparison. Unfortunately, much of what passes for popular culture in the present interests me much less and sometimes I have trouble keeping my mind focused on these things. Such disinterest can be perceived by others as a failing when it is really more an alteration of my attention. All things considered, establishing equilibrium about such things allows the enjoyment of the life that has been given to us in God's Providence. This is a talk that I have with myself every now and then.

George Santayana, also a conservative writer of the early 20<sup>th</sup> century, said "Those who cannot remember the past are condemned to fulfill it". There is no question that a knowledge of what has been tried before makes our choices for the present much more rational. Too much of what passes for political discussion in our lifetime is uninformed by any acknowledgement of historical fact.

It is a mistake, however, to over interpret the value of history to the present. If, for example, Ronald Reagan was daunted by the historical victories of the Russians over Napoleon and of the Soviets over Hitler, he would never have taken the steps that he did to defeat The Soviet Union in the Cold War. Thankfully, Reagan did not overextend historical analogy. One must be wary of judgments which make reference to historical precedent.

Perhaps there is a more edifying sense in which history serves to enrich a conservative view of life, and here I speak from personal conviction. It is in the realization that the real truths of history are those things for which men have always struggled. It is the knowledge that we are part of a continuity of earth-bound creatures, flawed by our own humanity yet blessed with God-given potential. Regarding this, I will close with some lines of Robert Frost from his long poem "The Black Cottage":

> Most of the change we think we see in life
> Is due to truths being in and out of favor.
> As I sit here, and oftentimes, I wish
> I could be monarch of a desert land
> I could devote and dedicate forever
> To the truths we keep coming back and back to . . . [113]

# EPILOGUE

This chronicle of my own journey has followed the powerful currents of the 20th century, observing them from the deep center stream and from the near bank shallows. The sun has set on that part of the river and many of those who navigated those waters, both public leaders and our own family members are now in darkness. For those of us who have passed into the next millennium, there is now the hope and the challenge of the unforeseen. Prediction, even with historical guideposts known, is inexact and cautionary. The specter of 9/11 has presented a new calculus into the hopeful world that emerged from the victory of the Cold War.

The unsettling fear that Islamic fundamentalism will succeed in wreaking chaos on our way of life is now foremost in the mindset of all who cherish the freedoms gained by Western civilization over the millennia. My own assessment however, is that the West will rise to this challenge and will prevail. But, as in the past defenses of freedom, there will be a cost. The fear that many have expressed over the loss of freedom caused by the encroachments of our own homeland security seem hyperbolic. If national security is abdicated, none of our laws mean anything. Fixing Medicare or Social Security is meaningless if America ceases to exist as it has in the past. The Patriot Act and other measures are necessary safeguards to protect "the last, best hope of mankind". As Supreme Court Justice Jackson said in 1949, "the constitution is not a suicide pact[114]".

Humility should guide any appeal to our God to protect us in our present endeavor[115]. After all, the radical Wahhabi's also pray to their God to provide success. It does not seem Providential however, for victory to come to those who espouse a 7th century philosophy and desire to erase the 1400 years of human striving and progress that intervenes. As the old saying goes, God helps those who help themselves. It is singularly up to us to ensure that the battle against terrorism is waged with certainty and with tenacity. Squishy moral equivalence must not daunt us on our way. Vexatious as they may be, the acknowledged abuses of Abu Ghraib are not the same as the beheading of innocent people.

On the personal and family level I also have an optimistic outlook for the years to come. The members of my family and the families of our close friends are honorable and virtuous people. Each generation fears that the next will not have the same opportunity or lifestyle that it has enjoyed. In this great country, where freedom and opportunity resides, that fear has not prevailed. Each of our generations seems to have done well and have provided greater opportunity for those who come after them.

Material wealth and comfort is not the only thing to which I speak. It is reassuring to know that sons and daughters will be able to provide economic security for themselves and their children but it is ultimately of secondary importance. None of us are born into a world of our own making. Our legacy is complicated by the sins of the past and the knowledge that a jealous God may visit "the iniquity of the fathers upon the children unto the third and fourth generation . . ."[116] Thus, in such a world, strength and resolve are required to find our way. I have detailed on these pages the heritage of the essentials of character through the generations of our family. Observing the development of our younger family members into mature men and women has been as satisfying to me as it had to be for the past parents of our line. Based on these realities, I have confidence and optimism for our future.

# ENDNOTES

## Prologue

[1]  CDC, National Center for Health Statistics, "Life Expectancy", Table 27.

[2]  Paul Johnson, "Modern Times", 1991, Harper-Collins, pg. 783. This detailed text is a must for anyone that wants an overview of the 20th century. Paul Johnson is a panoramic author who is not afraid to characterize what he reviews in subjective yet accurate terms.

[3]  Shakespeare, "Hamlet", II.i.316. I have restrained myself from quoting Shakespeare many times in this text in large part because the tendency could become excessive. This man, with a vocabulary of over 20,000 words had something to say about almost everything relating to the human drama and could say it better than any other could. He was "exceptional" in the truest sense of the word and may never be equaled.

[4]  Thomas Gray, "Elegy Written in a Country Churchyard", in the Norton Anthology of Poetry, pg. 609. Abraham Lincoln quoted a line from this poem in his biographical notes to John Howard Scripps, characterizing his early life as, "The short and simple annals of the poor."

## Chapter 1

[5]  My father kept a small diary with entries for all his missions over France and Germany. Each note included the date, destination,

weather and temperature conditions, and altitude. The amount of flak encountered was also included.

6   Some detail of these events was provided by a short entry into a newsletter of "The Last Man's Club", a WW I veterans club to which my grandfather belonged. He sent them a letter about the marriage and it appeared under the heading AIR MEDAL AND A BRIDE FOR SERGEANT LEONARD.

7   President Truman consulted his best military advisors to estimate the number of American deaths that would occur as a result of the looming invasion of the Japanese mainland. Based on the bloody and suicidal battles in the Pacific up until then, the numbers were as low as 60,000 and more generally closer to 1 million.

8   General George Marshall became the Secretary of State in the Truman Cabinet. The Marshall Plan for rebuilding Europe in 1948 cost $10.2 Billion over three years. P. Johnson, "Modern Times", pg. 440.

9   Moores Hill College became Evansville College in 1919 and then The University of Evansville in 1967. Joshua and Kara Leonard would later become graduates of this university.

10   According to the American Battle Monuments Commission, 26,255 Americans are buried in France from WWI and 30,426 from WWII. These 56,681 American liberators are scattered around their land in 11 different cemeteries.

11   There is much speculation as to whether Roosevelt's failing health contributed to his poor handling of the Soviet threat to Eastern Europe in the closing months of the war and including the Yalta Conference in Feb. 1945.

12   "Little Boxes" was composed by Malvina Reynolds. Pete Seeger was an old style leftist who joined the Communist Party in 1942 and then accompanied the Progressive Party's presidential candidate Henry Wallace in 1948. His other songs include "If I had a Hammer" and "Where Have All the Flowers Gone".

13   Orville H. Hubbard was the mayor in those days.

14   "In the right to earn one's bread, Lincoln insisted, blacks and whites were as equal as the word equal can mean-and when we remember that economic equality and economic opportunity were among

---

Lincoln's highest values . . . " see also pg 123 of Allen Guelzo, "Abraham Lincoln: Redeemer President", Eerdman's Publishing Co. April, 2003: "What wage labor promised was a potential for betterment and self improvement which the static, rigid system of both yeoman agrarianism and plantation slavery utterly lacked".

## Chapter 2

[15] In the same year of our founding, 1776, Adam Smith wrote "The Wealth of Nations". He explained the operation of a free market place so simply that it has been forgotten by many in the public since and certainly by more than a few of the wise men known as economists.

## Chapter 3

[16] It is of interest that the three prior awakenings preceded wars. The American Revolution, the Civil War and the First World War were all preceded by increased religious activity. In times of stress, America seems to turn to Providence for guidance. What secular guidance was offered prior to the Vietnam War is not as clear.

[17] Paul Johnson, "Modern Times", pg. 628

[18] Seymour Hersh, "The Dark Side of Camelot", Publisher Back Bay Books, Sept. 1998.

[19] For an extensive examination of achievement and intelligence in this period and others see, Richard Herrnstein and Charles Murray, "The Bell Curve", Published by Free Press, Sept. 1994.

[20] The founders anticipated the divides of "factions" but probably did not foresee the rise of "parties". They might have been surprised by the development of permanent political parties in the manifest way that they came about. Nevertheless, refer to Federalist No. 10 by James Madison, "An Extensive Republic a Remedy for Mischief's of Faction", in The Federalist, Edited and introduced by Robert Scigliano, Published by the Modern Library, 2000.

[21] James McPherson, "The Battle Cry of Freedom", pg 854, Published by the Oxford University Press, 1988.

22  Bernard Goldberg, himself a media person previously employed at ABC News, found himself *persona non grata* when he wrote a book detailing the bias of the news media. "Bias", publisher Perennial Currents, Jan. 2003

23  Douglas Kinnaird, "President Eisenhower and Strategic Management", Publisher Lexington, 1977.

24  The comparison with the Gore-Bush election is of interest. Richard Nixon had just as much, if not more reason to challenge the results of his defeat, there being suspected irregularities in several states. He decided that a protracted legal challenge would not be good for the country and did the honorable thing and conceded the election. What a contrast to the drawn out battle over "hanging chads" of 2000.

25  Polls taken at the time of the Nixon-Kennedy debates showed differences between the television audience who thought Kennedy won and the radio audience who thought Nixon won. See Prof. Patrick N. Allitt, "The History of the United States", 2nd Ed. Part VII, lecture 74; The Teaching Company, 4151 Lafayette Center Dr., Chantilly, VA 20151.

## Chapter 4

26  The bailout used the reasoning that since government regulation contributed to Chrysler's troubles that it was fair to ask for a government subsidy to save the company and its jobs. The end justified the means as it has in other issues. The present protectionist legislation for the aging steel industry supported by the Bush administration is similar in kind. Why everyone (taxpayers) should be punished to help some specific companies or industries is a perennial question of liberal democracy.

27  The black rioting resulted in 43 deaths and required mobilization of the Michigan National Guard. President Johnson deployed the 18th Airborne Corps. These were among the worst civil insurrections of American history. "Report of the National Advisory Commission on Civil Disorders". Washington D.C., 56.

28  Michael Barone, "Politics in Michigan", published Oct. 1, 1954. See Harvard Crimson Online.

[29] McCullough was sheriff and clerk of the McLean County Circuit Court in Bloomington, IL. The letter to his daughter was dated December 23, 1862.

[30] "Friday Focus: Birth of a Student Movement", the Michigan Daily, February 13, 2002.

[31] "This Week in Daily History", the Michigan Daily, Dec 11, 2002 about December 11, 1967.

[32] Jeff Leen, "The Vietnam Protests: When Worlds Collided", Washington Post, Sept. 27, 1999, pg. A1.

[33] A long and thoughtful discussion of this period is available in print or online. Michael Jay Friedman, "Congress, the President, and the Battle or Ideas: Vietnam Policy, 1965-1969. Essays in History, Vol. 41, 1999, Published by the Corcoran Department of History at the University of Virginia.

[34] Victor Davis Hanson examines the Tet offensive in detail, a marine victory he considers one of the most successful in U.S. military history. "Carnage and Culture: Landmark Battles in the Rise of Western Powers", pg 389, published by Anchor Books, September, 2002.

[35] "Clean for Gene: Eugene McCarthy and the Presidential Election of 1968", online @ www.ncs.pvt.k12.va.us/ryerbury/wes/wes.htm

## Chapter 5

[36] "About the School", Wayne State University School of Michigan, online @www.med.wayne.edu/about-the-school/htm

[37] "About the Wayne State University School of Medicine", the Detroit News/FREEP, February 22, 2000.

## Chapter 6

[38] It is interesting to compare the many "rights" that those on the left have conjured over the years with the conception of rights that were considered by the founders of our country. The Declaration of Independence states that the inalienable rights are life, liberty and the pursuit of happiness. Just these three are included and they are

granted by God and not man. The constitutional compromise that became the Bill of Rights (the first ten amendments) limited the powers of government in the lives of individual citizens. They did not compel citizens to do something like the "rights" crowd now wants and they are not directed to group entitlements.

[39] Mao Tse-Tung, "In memory of Norman Bethune", Selected works of Mao Tse-Tung, Foreign Languages Press, Peking, 1967, Vol. II, pg. 337-8.

[40] "Every communist must grasp the truth; political power grows out of the barrel of a gun." Ibid., pg. 224. "The seizure of power by armed force, the settlement of the issue by war, is the central task and the highest form of revolution. This Marxist-Leninist principle of revolution holds good universally, for China and for all other countries." Ibid. pg. 219.

[41] Pol Pot, Time Magazine, August 23-30, 1999. Vol. 154, No. 718.

[42] The Old Testament; Genesis 33:3.

[43] Mona Charon, "Useful Idiots: How Liberals Got It Wrong in the Cold War and Still Blame America First", Regnery Publishing, February, 2003.

[44] Aristotle, "The Nicomachean Ethics", Oxford World's Classics, Oxford University Press, June, 1998.

## Chapter 7

[45] Controversy exists over whether Churchill actually said this, although it is commonly attributed to him. Apparently, variations of this quotation are attributed to several others, including Georges Clemenceau (insert communist), George Bernard Shaw (insert socialist), Benjamin Disraeli, and others.

[46] Detroit General Hospital started out as Detroit Receiving Hospital in 1915. In 1965 the name was changed to Detroit General. Then in 1980 the hospital moved to its new location in the Detroit Medical Center and reclaimed the name of Detroit Receiving Hospital. The current facility is a 320 bed acute care and Trauma, level 1 hospital.

47  See "Academic Emergency Medicine, Wayne State University-Past, Present and Future", online @www.dmc.org/em/25ᵗʰ/25th-presentation_files/outline.htm.

48 See "Detroit Receiving Hospital", 4201 St. Antoine, Department of Medicine, Detroit, MI 48202.

## Chapter 8

49  See Dickinson County Healthcare System, 1721 S. Stephenson Ave., Iron Mountain MI 49801 or online @ www.dchs.org.

50  Paul Johnson, "Modern Times", Ibid, pg 653.

51  Carter's speech of July 15, 1979 can be found online @www.fritannica.com/elections/pri/Q00016.html.

52  For a longer discussion of this entire period, see "US-Iranian Relations and the Hostage Crisis", online @www.geocities.com/bandyh2001/iran/index2.html.

53  CNN Report, October 11, 2002, online @www.cnn.com/2002/WORLD/Europe/10/11carter.nobel.

54  "Ex-President Jimmy Carter Slams 'Arrogant' US Foreign Policy", Published by Agence France Presse, November 16, 2002.

55  Edwin J. Feulner, jr., "Morning in America-Reagan Rebuilt the Presidency", Policy Review, spring 1989, The Reagan Years Published by the Heritage Foundation.

56  Dinesh D'Sousa, Ronald Reagan-How an Ordinary Man Became an Extraordinary Leader", Published by The Free Press, 1997, pg 135 and 191.

57  Named after a fictitious place in James Hilton's novel "Lost Horizon" (1933), Shangri-La was the name given by FDR to the presidential retreat in Frederick Co., Maryland. This was located in the Catoctin Mountains in what was known prior to 1942 as The Camp Catoctin Mtn. Park. It was then renamed Camp David by Dwight Eisenhower in 1953. This place has been the site of many high level meetings, including the planning of the Normandy invasion with Winston Churchill in WW II, and the Camp David Accords between Anwar Sadat and Menachem Begin in 1978.

## Chapter 9

[58] Rudyard Kipling, "Christmas in India".

[59] For a discussion of these matters, see; Prof. Luke Timothy Johnson, "Early Christianity: The Experience of the Divine", Part II-Lecture 16,'Meals Are Where the Magic Is', Ibid. The Teaching Company.

[60] Mark Bowden, "Blackhawk Down", Published by Penguin Books, February 28, 2000.

## Chapter 10

[61] Dinesh D'Sousa, Ibid, pg 251.

[62] George Washington, "The Farewell Address", online @www.gwpapers.virginia.edu/farewell/transcript.html.

[63] Alexis de Tocqueville, "Democracy in America", Everyman's Library, Reprint Edition, May, 1994.

[64] Johnson, Paul, Ibid, pg 435.

[65] Ibid. pg 433.

[66] "Winston Churchill and the Sinews of Peace Address", March 5, 1946, Westminster College, Fulton, Missouri, online @www.hpol.org/Churchill/.

[67] Robert A. Devine, "Eisenhower and the Cold War", pg 20, Published by Oxford University Press, 1981.

[68] Paul Johnson, Ibid, pg 461-2.

[69] Peter Robinson, "Morning Again in America", the Wall Street Journal, Monday, June 7, 2004, A20.

[70] Anyone who doubts Reagan's ability to perceive these issues clearly should read, "Reagan in His Own Hand-The Writings of Ronald Reagan That Reveal His Revolutionary Vision for America", Ed. K. Skinner, A. Anderson, M. Anderson, Published by The Free Press, 2001.

[71] Associated Press, "Thatcher Lauds Reagan on Cold War Effort", June 11, 2004.

[72] Stephanie Courtois, Nicolas Werth, et al., "The Black Book of Communism", Harvard University Press.

73 Matt Pottinger, "New Edition of the Tiananmen Papers Dredges Up Details of Military's Actions", The Wall Street Journal, August 23, 2004.

74 "Downside Legacy at Two Degrees of President Clinton Section: Behind the Treason Allegations Subsection: Sandy Berger", Free Republic, August 9, 1999, online @ www.freerepublic.com/forum/a37c46da04c3a.htm.

75 "The Berlin Wall", online @ http://userpage.chemie.fu-berlin.de/BIW/wall,html.

76 John J. Miller, "Communism's Victims Await Their Memorial", The Wall Street Journal, May 26, 2004.

## Chapter 11

77 Christine Gorman, "Cover Story: Sizing Up the Sexes", January 20, 1992, Time Magazine.

78 The Greek city states fought horrific wars among themselves, but during the Olympic Games, they came together in the spirit of competition. See Jeremy McInerney, Professor at the University of Pennsylvania, and lectures prepared for The Teaching Company, Ibid, "The Olympics: From Ancient Greece to Athens, Part I and Part II.

79 Using a properly positioned catheter, a cardiology sub-specialist called an electrophysiologist, destroys the identified pathway using a low frequency electrical impulse. Because the pathways are very near to normal structures, there is always a risk of damage to the conducting system of the heart which might then require a life-long pacemaker. When properly and successfully done however, this treatment can be life-saving and marvelous. It can "cure" patients of their malady and leave them free of taking medication or treatment for the rest of their lives.

80 "U.S. Supreme Court Rules on University of Michigan Cases", University of Michigan News Service, October 20, 2003. Online @ www.umich.edu/Releases/2003/Jun03/supremedourt.html.

81 Shelby Steele, "The Conundrum of Quotas", the Wall Street Journal, June 6, 2001.

# Chapter 12

[82] Winston Churchill, "The Gathering Storm",

[83] Winston Churchill, Ibid, 1939, pg 171.

[84] Bernard Trainor, "Oral History of the Gulf War", Frontline, 2001, online @ www.pbs.org/wgbh/pages/frontline/gulf/oral/trainor/7.html.

[85] Ibid, pg 4.

[86] Victor Davis Hanson, "The soul of Battle", pg 411, Published by the Free Press, 1999.

[87] The Oxford Dictionary of Quotations", 3rd Edition, Published by Book Club Associates, 1980, pg 251.

[88] John Dilbeck, "The Order of the Garter", online @ www.johndilbeck.com/geneology/orderofthe garter.html.

[89] John Lancaster "Les Aspin Supports Allowing Homosexuals in Military if They Keep Orientation Private", The Washington Post, June 23, 1993, pg 2.

[90] Tony Mauro, "Race Factor Tilts the Scales of Public Opinion", USA Today, February 5, 1997.

[91] Robert P. George, "The Clinton Puzzle: Why Do Liberals Love Him So?" the Wall Street Journal, Opinion Page.

[92] "A Guide to the Monica Lewinsky Story", the Coffee Shop Times, updated July 8, 2001, online @ www.coffeeshoptimes.com/monica.html.

[93] "The Articles of Impeachment Against William Jefferson Clinton", HS 122 Document, online @www.virginiawestern.edu/vwhansd/HIS122/Clinton_Impeachment.html.

[94] "How do we Know that Iraq Tried to Assassinate President H.W. Bush?" a report from the Department of Justice website, online@ www.hnn.us/articles/1000.html.

[95] Seymour Hersh, "A Case Not Closed", the New Yorker, November 11, 1993.

[96] See "Of Lies and WMD", Review and Outlook, the Wall Street Journal, July 12, 2004, pgA16.

[97] Hillary Clinton, "Living History", Published by Simon and Schuster, June 9, 2003,

[98] Bill Clinton, "My Life", Published by Knopf, June 22, 2004.

[99] Sidney Blumenthal, "The Clinton Wars", Published by Farrar, Straus and Giroux, May 20, 2003.

# Chapter 13

[100] Edward Gibbon, "The History of the Decline and Fall of the Roman Empire", pg 99, Penguin Books; Abridged Edition, January 2, 2001.
[101] This and other Burn's selections can be found in "The Norton Anthology of Poetry", Fourth Edition, pg694, Norton Publishers, 1996.

# Chapter 14

[102] Kahlil Gibran, "The Prophet", pg16, Published by Alfred A. Knopf, 1968.
[103] Aristotle in his book "The Politics", written in 335 B.C., precedes Locke with the statement that "man is by nature a political animal". Politics indicates the Polis, or city state, without which man would be bereft of humanity. Within the partnerships of the family and the Polis, man is completed. "For just as man is the best of the animals when completed, when separated from law and adjudication he is the worst of all".
[104] This is not Ecclesiastes of the Old Testament but Ecclesiasticus of the Apocrypha.
[105] Othello, II,iii, 315: OK, I promised to limit Shakespeare quotations, but I cannot help myself!
[106] Aristotle, the Nicomachean Ethics, Ibid. above.

# Chapter 15

[107] The Declaration of Independence can be obtained from many sources. The document divides into four basic parts: First is the declaration of the intent to "dissolve the political bands" of the former colonies; Second is the rationale and statement of why "governments are instituted among men" and what natural truths are "self-evident"; Third is a long list of grievances against the crown; The last is the formal declaration by the assembled representatives that on behalf of "the good people of these colonies, [they]solemnly publish and declare" their independence from Great Britain. The quote in the present text comes from the final sentence of the document.

[108] "The Federalist", edited by Robert Scigliano, Ibid. above. Professor Scigliano teaches this text and his introduction and comments are detailed and lucid.

[109] Ibid, "The Oxford Dictionary of Quotations", pg 276.

[110] Victor Davis Hanson and John Heath, "Who Killed Homer? The Demise of Classical Education and the Recovery of Greek Wisdom", Published by Free Press, April 7, 1998.

[111] Russell Kirk, "The Conservative Mind: From Burke to Eliot", pg 37, Regnery Publishing; 7th Edition, 1995.

[112] Russell Kirk, "The Politics of Prudence", Chapter II: 'Ten Conservative Principles' Published by ISI Books, October, 1998.

[113] The full poem can be found in "The Poetry of Robert Frost Edited by Edward Connery Lathem, pg 55, Published by Holt, Rhinehart and Winston, 1969.

## Epilogue

[114] There is much heated discussion over the legal specifics of the Jackson ruling: See David Corn, "The 'Suicide Pact ' Mystery", in Slate, Friday, January 4, 2002 and also George P. Fletcher, "The Cliché That 'The Constitution is Not a Suicide Pact': Why It is Actually Pro-, Not Anti-, Civil Liberties, online @http://writ.news.fin.dlaw.com/commentary/20030107_fletcher.html.

Personally, I cannot get excited about the so-called abuses of the Patriot Act when I know that Lincoln revoked Habeas Corpus during the Civil War, Wilson deported communists and anarchists during the First War, and FDR detained the Japanese Americans in camps in WW II. As bad as all that was, we have lived through it. Civil liberties seem more threatened by those who twist or ignore the constitution in other ways today than by the Patriot Act, which pales in comparison.

[115] Lincoln's words in the Second Inaugural give admonition to those that invoke God to help them win in war: "It may seem strange that any men should dare to ask a just God's assistance in wringing their bread from the sweat of other men's faces".

[116] Exodus 20:5.

# INDEX